MORAL EDUCATION / FIVE LECTURES

Moral Education *Five Lectures*

JAMES M. GUSTAFSON / RICHARD S. PETERS

LAWRENCE KOHLBERG / BRUNO BETTELHEIM

KENNETH KENISTON / *With an Introduction by*

Nancy F. and Theodore R. Sizer

Harvard University Press
Cambridge, Massachusetts
1970

Distributed in Great Britain by Oxford University Press, London
Library of Congress Catalog Card Number 74-128149
SBN 674-58660-3
Printed in the United States of America

CONTENTS

MORAL EDUCATION / FIVE LECTURES

INTRODUCTION / *Nancy F. Sizer and Theodore R. Sizer*

Morality is embedded in all formal education. The experience of schooling changes all children, some for the better, some unhappily. Often the changes are hardly the ones planned by the teacher or even apparent to him. Nonetheless, teachers must carry a major burden, along with the family, in helping children to meet and deal justly with moral problems.

There was a time when "moral problems" were recognized as the core of formal schooling. These problems were cast in sectarian religious molds, and youngsters were "taught" moral conduct. Oliver Twist got his moral lessons from Mr. Bumble, as did the boys at Rugby from Thomas Arnold and Williams men from Mark Hopkins. There was an appealing simplicity to their task: "right" and "wrong" were clear and undisputed and were to be learned directly. If one could recite righteous precepts, one would practice them— or so the crude pedagogy of the day implied. The nine-teenth-century teacher sermonized, and his charges listened (sometimes) and learned (some things). Crude and philo-sophically simpleminded though the sermonizing tradition may be, it had its effect. The Christian gentleman ideal in England had and still has a profound effect on a sector of British and Commonwealth society, particularly its leadership. And the moralisms of the prairie have a strong hold on the large remnant of Middle America. Nixon's "forgotten American" learned much from simple sermonizing. For a class of people it worked; it took hold. *But was it moral?*

The answer is a qualified no; sermonizing denies individual autonomy, which, with justice, lies at the heart of a new morality. While abstract morality is surely no more or less complex than it has always been (God knows that Dickens' slums were no better than ours), teaching toward it in any profound way is far more complicated than earlier schoolmasters may have believed. It was to explore the various deep problems within "moral education'" that five essays were given as a lecture series at the Harvard Graduate School of Education in the spring of 1968. They make the point of complexity all too well: The prevailing impression for

the schoolteacher who reads these essays is that the
attempt to teach morality *must* be made by teachers, that they
must approach their task vigorously and yet carefully,
aware of all its intricacies and dangers, and that, considering
the state of the world we are in, where *im*morality can carry
such a high price tag for us all, all teachers of morality
had better be successful—very soon. The "morality" to be
taught is more than a litany from McGuffey and infinitely
more subtle and complex.

While the essays give many reasons to point up the
complexity and difficulty of "teaching" morality, they all agree
that it must be taught nonetheless. There is no "morality-
free" school, no valueless teaching. Any interpersonal
experience contains a moral element, virtually by definition,
and a classroom is no exception. The authors all appear to
agree that the old "bag of virtues" approach, to use Professor Kohlberg's phrase, is discredited; no longer can we list
a group of desirable qualities within a person or objective
moral "truths" about the world and expect children to take
them over intact. The fear—whether of an unjust God, a harsh
father or king, or a life of want unless one worked terribly
hard—which underlaid that "old morality" is no longer
a large part of life in America. But the need for some sort of
morality is with us still. Moral autonomy, the independent
arrival at a conviction of one's own accountability toward
one's fellow men, the rational and emotional acceptance of
justice as the most proper atmosphere in which all
individuals can flourish, including even one's secret self—this
is the "new morality" toward which we are to guide
ourselves and other people.

The stress on eventual autonomy and independence is
what has confused matters for many of us. For we tend to
regard childhood as a time of pleasure, of freedom, of
"doing one's own thing"; and many of us regard the "real"
world, the world of adulthood, as a place where "reality" can
prove very repressive indeed. Yet the road to more
sophisticated moral thinking, according to Professors Kohlberg
and Bettelheim in particular, is precisely the *opposite:*

4

the child, having been fearful of repression, can later become oblivious to it as a guide toward moral thinking, and unless other forms of guidance are offered, he will in fact have no guidance, no reason for morality, at all. "Relative" morality, what Professor Bettelheim calls the "sometimes no and sometimes yes" approach, can seem honest and sensible to adults—especially adults who are wary about "playing God" and who are trying to encourage children to learn to make their own judgments. But it can seem like hypocrisy to adolescents, especially as they discover that no can turn to yes when enough pressure is applied, and especially as they observe their parents and teachers, "permissive" in theory, turning authoritarian very rapidly when they are frightened, angry, or tired. Some form of "absolute" morality, then, seems to be required, even if one guides one's charges toward it in a flexible and sensitive manner.

Implicit in the criticism of the present teaching of morality in America's schools on the part of all of the authors of this volume is this point: The "old morality" can and should be scrapped, but has a "new morality" really been put in its place? Can one take on the commitment of teaching, any more than the commitment of parenthood, without an understanding of these relatively fixed principles which underlie all our lives? Can we dare to place ourselves in contact with children if we do not have purposes for them, if we do not have dreams for them and plans for helping them to get there? Clearly the strict adherence to a "code" is out of date; but equally harmful is "planlessness" or a new "creative code." And a teacher who offers these three alternatives as his only ones is immoral: he is wasting the children's time.

His plan must involve justice. All other principles, like impartiality and respect for others, and all other human qualities, like self-giving and commitment, relate to justice. It is the "absolute" standard toward which we might all, despite our many varying values, strive. Constant comparison of one's "lesser" values against the standard of moral justice—values like honesty, self-interest, love for one's children, freedom—does not mean to deny them but only

5

to keep them in some kind of perspective. In some times
and places these "lesser" values have come, by custom and
even by law, to have too great a power over men's lives,
to have impeded the justice which was due to them. Only
constant review, constant adjustment, can prevent this
from happening, and the teacher of morality must try to
introduce this process of review and adjustment not
only into his own life but into another's.

How to do this? This is where, although the ultimate goal
is "absolute," the means to the end are flexible. One starts,
as Bettelheim puts it, "where the child is." One looks at his
age, the pressures upon him, how far he has learned to
trust life. One notices the kinds of responses within him—fear
of harm, or loss of another's love, or loss of one's sense of
place in the world, or loss of one's self-respect—which
seem to make him think and act in "just" ways.

Taking all of these states of morality, one builds on each
of them in the way appropriate to the individual child.
One uses firmness, affection, respect, where they are needed
and appropriate, but, even where one uses one sort of
guidance, one tries to expose the child to other sorts of moral
thinking, to moral imperatives which seem to make other
people act. If these other examples of "morality at work" are
close enough to the child's own conscious or unconscious attitudes, then understanding them will cause him to
consider adopting them, and eventually to try to adopt
them. Thus rational exposure, whether by discussion or example, to superior forms of moral thinking, if these forms are
near enough to the child's own thinking to seem accessible
to him, will in fact make the child more aware of the various
elements involved in justice, and in time will make him
more just himself.

This is, obviously, a subtle and difficult pedagogical task.
After judging his students accurately, which is never
easy, a teacher must be prepared to use different responses
toward each one, and this in the presence of the others.
He must explain, when challenged, in words which seem
honest to himself and yet understandable to the student, why

he acts as he does. For the student who, at seventeen, still refers to teachers as either "nice" or "mean" one must *act* "nice" but still begin to introduce to the student some notion of *self*-respect, some feeling that one can grow for one's *own* reasons, and not merely in response to the affection of the "nice" teacher.

What of the students who have self-respect, who are not really responsive either to fear of repression or to fear of the loss of the affection of a "nice" teacher? For those students, discussions among each other, based either on decisions which they must make themselves or on others available to the class from history or literature, are probably the best ways for students to come to know both their own values and others which are more justice-oriented than their own. It is in this sense that a rational approach, by providing an awareness of alternatives and an ever-increasing sensitivity to the human condition, can lead students to feel, in Professor Peters's term, "on the inside" of morality: not only to know, but also to act, in moral ways.

But morality cannot remain merely an intellectual *morality* exercise; it must be put to the test, and children must see it *put to* put to the test by themselves and by others around them in *the test* and out of the schools. And this is why Professor Kohlberg says that justice cannot be taught in unjust schools, why Professor Keniston urges us to correct injustice rather than to learn to live with it, to control technology rather than to let it warp us, why Professor Peters urges us not to forget or ignore the lessons which we as humans have learned, not to throw out the whole humane tradition in romantic protest against some repressive parts in it.

Morality *is* put to the test every day in schools, and we teachers are often found wanting in it. While we doubt the value in giving grades, they're there anyway, often to the terror of the young. We put up with practices which we know are immoral because we don't want to get in trouble. All too often we don't really think through what is best for the young until pressured, and then we yield to that pressure. How can we expect them to understand this? We are often not self-giving; and at times we are too self-giving, encouraging dependence on us or slavish imitation of our model on children who should be learning their own independence, developing their own models.

Repression is the most commonly criticized form of immorality in schools, especially by the middle class, but it is not by any means the only one: many teachers, like Charlie Brown, are wishy-washy, and cannot see that a fierce "revolutionary" and long-standing commitment to justice is the only way for any adult to maintain his moral superiority over the young, and without this *kind* of superiority, there is no real basis for authority.

Yet the shrinking from positions of authority is another form of immorality, we think; it seeks to avoid the problem, to avoid one's responsibility to children and to this form of improvement of justice in our society. Many teachers and principals today are what Professor Kohlberg would call "Stage 5 thinkers"; they know that things as they are in their schools are legal, but not always moral, yet they lack either the temerity or the patience to change them. They "drop out," physically, mentally, or both. And the atmosphere generated by their disappointment with themselves infects the school and infects thinking about schooling in general. It leads to carping, do-nothing thinking, hardly a good step toward any moral values at all. This is the greatest harm we can do to the moral development of the young: Not even to believe in the fundamental justice of these institutions which we have freely entered ourselves—the family, society, schools. Of course these institutions are not perfect, but if we are committed to them, we should reform them *and* defend them.

Reform of injustice, whether of unjust schools or other injustices, is something which must be done and is something we can do *with* our children. In the process, we can feel again their question, "Why be moral at all?", which every child needs to ask of his mother, every generation of its elders. We can remember, too, the agony involved in being small and helpless, the perception that every spanking is "being beaten up," every adjustment is threatening, every judgment full of terror. We can come to see how, for the

young, repression and exploitation of anyone fits into
this picture of their own helplessness. And when we remember
again how we too once had to try to piece together the
world somehow, bit by bit, we can perhaps appreciate better
the child's sensitivity toward hypocrisy. Surely the teacher
who extols democracy in the beginning of the lesson but refuses to explain his reasons for something at its end is
open to question. If he can see these questions in his students'
eyes, if he considers himself "accountable" to them and
tries to address himself to them, he is more credible both as a
teacher and as a human being.

What can the students learn from teachers, as together they
set about reforming the admittedly imperfect schools? The
students, through discussions of the changes needed,
can come to see these "improvements" against a final
goal of responsible autonomy, and, through decisions about
the tactics needed, can come to see what part raw power,
sensitivity toward others, and persuasion can have in any
efforts at reform. The teacher who cares about a "new world"
which is not only different from the old but also better by
being more just will naturally question hypocrisy and
unclear reasoning on the part of his students, or unjust
methods used in the name of "just" ends, no matter where or
how. For these teachers, "revolution" will be a means which
could lead to unjust *or* just ends; but terror has only
immoral consequences, both on the terrorized and on the
terrorizer, and in various contexts these distinctions could be
made clear to the young, even without a "sermon."

So teachers and children can learn about morality from
each other. By our analysis of our students' needs, by our skill
and persistence in addressing ourselves to them, by the
atmosphere conducive to moral growth which we try to
provide for them in the classroom and in the school building,
by the discussions we are willing to facilitate between them
or to engage in with them, and by our own stance toward
society and the injustice which we see within it, whether we
are facile or ardent, determined or despairing, we can and
do influence our students' moral growth. And, despite
its dangers, it is a job which can—and must—be done well.

EDUCATION FOR MORAL RESPONSIBILITY

James M. Gustafson

Meno asks Socrates, "Can you tell me, Socrates, whether virtue is acquired by teaching or by practice; or if neither by teaching nor practice, then whether it comes to man by nature, or in what other way?" [1] This reminds us not only of the venerable age of the question of moral education but also of its complexity. A normative question of the highest order is involved: what virtue or virtues are to be acquired? There is a pedagogical question of how virtue is acquired which runs into questions of man's nature and even into religious questions (at the end of the *Meno,* Socrates entertains the possibility that virtue is a gift of the gods.) An institutional question is involved, namely, who is responsible in the social order for the acquiring of virtue on the part of the young?

In our time the complexities are compounded. The question of moral education has become more inclusive than the question of how virtues are to be acquired. Less consensus exists on what characteristics constitute the morally commendable life, for our culture is heir not only of the Greek tradition but of the Jewish and Christian ones also. There is a radical questioning of the traditional values and norms, and of their religious and philosophical sources, not only because of exposure to still other historic traditions but also because of the inadequacy of much of traditional morality to cope with the possibilities and problems of modern life. Our circumstances for facing the question of moral education are very different from those of ancient Athens, of an even more ancient Sinai, and of a later Galilee.

In this essay the following procedure will be followed, even though it excludes many facets of the subject matter and simplifies many technical and complex issues. First, moral action and the moral actor will be briefly characterized in a way that functions both descriptively and normatively. Second, some salient aspects of that characterization of the

moral actor will be briefly developed in order to suggest
some kinds of education that might have commendable effects
upon the moral life. Finally, some observations about the
role of religion in moral education are made.

MORAL ACTION AND MORAL ACTORS

Professor F. A. Olafson correctly discerns a common strain
in continental existentialist and phenomenological ethical
theories, on the one hand, and contemporary Anglo-
American moral philosophy on the other, in that both are
progressively developing the idea of moral autonomy in
contrast with the idea of absolute moral truth.[2] The idea of
moral autonomy is not only prominent in academic
ethical theory; it is also consistent with what contemporary
persons are claiming for themselves and with the vision many
ordinary people have of what normatively the moral life
ought to be. In religious morality this trend is dramatically
illustrated in the contemporary Roman Catholic church.
Whereas in its history the Catholic church has institutionalized a certain set of moral truths, and with a juridical
ecclesiastical authority has demanded obedience to these
moral truths, today many Catholics are calling for a revision
of this legal and magisterial model in favor of a Christian
ethics of responsive and creative action for human
well-being. The new Catholic ideal of the moral person is not
so much one who is free from the strains of sin through
scrupulous obedience to the eternal moral truths of the
church's teaching as it is one who is motivated to be freely
self-giving in service to others in the world. The new
vision is one of greater autonomy: The person is responsible
for discerning what is required in given circumstances;
the Church becomes more the enabler of freedom than
the prescriber of conduct and judge of moral mistakes.

Human being are moral actors; we have experiences which

can loosely be called moral before we are ever formally taught anything about ethics. We respond to one another, to rules and patterns of authority, to events, to institutional powers in ways which we judge to be right and wrong and in ways which enhance or detract from human well-being. We are initiators, whose purposive words and whose use of energy, money, and other forms of power have some beneficial or harmful effects on other persons and on the course of events. We are from our earliest years deciding, commending, evaluating, and exerting influence and power about matters which involve moral values. The subject matter of moral education, whatever it might be, is not alien to the ordinary experiences of persons.

Moral life can be conceived of primarily in terms of action and interaction; persons can be conceived of as responders and as initiators. The relations and interactions between persons, or between institutionalized powers subject to human decisions, are not absolutely determined nor are they merely a matter of chance. They provide the occasions for moral action. They provide the interstices, the gaps between self and other, between present and future, which are traversed by human actions. The person who acts is not an indeterminate self: what he does and what he becomes by his doing are in part determined by what he has previously become. The other, whether it is a person, or an institution, or an event, also has done some determinate characteristics; one responds to what the other now is, or, more precisely, what one now perceives, understands, and interprets it to be. But both the self and the other have a degree of malleability, alterability; they are subject to change, to direction, and to resistance in the processes of interaction. Persons respond and initiate responses; they intervene in a course of events or a state of affairs to alter what is, or to preserve what is, and to give some direction to what is going to be. Persons act to give some determination to the future (their

own and others') in accord with intentions and purposes
that they have. Persons affect the course of events and give
some shape to the states of affairs by their intentional
behavior.

Moral actions are interventions through the exercise of
some form of power in accord with intentions, rules, and ends,
which are subject to qualitative judgments of good or bad,
or right or wrong. Moral values and moral obligations are
involved in actions; one acts for the sake of altering the state
of affairs in such a way that there is a preservation of or
increment in what is morally valued by the person or by the
community. One judges what he should do, or what he
ought to do, in the light of responsibilities to himself, to
others, and in religious morality, to God. What we seek in
"moral education" is to develop or influence persons in such
a way that their action is morally responsible.

Responsible moral action involves at least these salient
features. There is an evaluative assessment of the circumstances in which action takes place, an interpretation of what
the possible courses of action are in the situation. There
is reflection about what ends are to be sought, what intentions
are to direct behavior, what rules are to be followed; there
is, in short, a process of moral decision-making. There is
reflection about the person's moral commitments, loyalties,
and beliefs, and what light they shed on the circumstances, on
the proper decision and on the appropriate means of action.
There is the person as an agent, his unconscious determinants,
character, dispositions, attitudes, and emotions, as well
as his capacities to make rational judgments. There is a
"willing" determination of capacities and powers in order to
achieve intentions. A more precise and detailed elaboration of
this outline is not necessary for the purpose of this essay.[3]

The practical interest in moral education in this general
view is to make possible the development of persons who
are capable of responsible moral action. We want them to

accept their autonomy and to exercise their capacities to be
agents in the ongoing processes of human interaction. We
want them to accept moral accountability for what they do
and to accept responsibility for others: for persons to
whom they are significantly related and for the course of
events and states of affairs of which they are part. We want
them to be agents and initiators, not merely passive reactors,
in the lifestream of which they are part.[4] This sort of
person is to be preferred to the excessively scrupulous keeper
of a clean conscience, who seeks authoritative moral prescrip-
tions from some person or institution by which to govern his
conduct, and thus denies his autonomy, and incidentally
is probably a boring and ineffectual member of the human
community.

SALIENT ASPECTS OF PERSONS WHO ACT

Persons, not acts, are subject to education. But certain
aspects of persons which seem to be involved in moral action
are more susceptible to the intentional influences of education than are others, and there are no doubt different ways
of learning and teaching that are more effective for some
aspects of "moral selfhood" than for others. Several aspects of
what we shall loosely call "moral selfhood" are indicated
in order to raise the question of which are teachable in some
sense and how they might be "taught." The exploratory
character of this essay makes what follows more a matter of
stating an agenda for further work than a detailed and precise
discussion.

1. One aspect of persons who act morally is sometimes
called "unconscious motivation"; that is, those presumably
"real" determinants of behavior which underlie and often
are different from the reasons we give for our actions. Some
say that the determination of the unconscious is final
and absolute and that therefore the notion of responsibility is

a mistake. Others say that the unconscious is not really involved in moral conduct *per se,* since it is not subject to conscious purpose and intention; for example, Paul Ricoeur suggests that all we can do is to consent to unconscious motives. At least they affect some characteristics of moral agents. A loving disposition, for example, is difficult to have if one has been unloved in childhood; or moral indignation and hostility to social evils might be sublimated forms of hostility to one's parents. Are "unconscious motives" subject to education? Does psychotherapy become part of "moral training," at least in some cases?

2. One's beliefs or convictions about certain moral values, about what is morally right and good, what is to be preferred, condition the sort of person one becomes. Beliefs or convictions can be stated at various levels of generality, and each person cannot necessarily, upon request, recite a credo of moral values. Nor is it suggested that a person's statement of moral beliefs absolutely determines what he does in each situation. There are beliefs about God, about the ultimate course of events, about persons to be emulated, about principles to be used to test one's proposed actions, about particular rules to be obeyed, and many more.[5] Further, *believing* is not always the same; there is more or less consent, assent, passion, loyalty involved in different persons; there is more or less doubt, skepticism, and even cynicism. What moral beliefs are worthy of being "taught?" Is "believing" teachable?

3. Character, habits, disposition, and attitudes all suggest persistent "traits" of persons. A great deal of dispute exists about the use of these terms, and this is not the place to sort out all of the complexities. A suitable notion of "character" for our purposes is that which marks "the sort of man" one is, the persistence of identity that makes us expect some consistency in a person's moral judgments, attitudes, and actions. A person's most persistent tendencies to

judge and act in certain ways, as these are inferred from observations of his behavior, mark his character. Disposition can be used to refer to tendencies to respond and behave in certain particular ways; they are bearings toward others and toward events and affairs of the world. Thus we can speak of loving or hopeful dispositions. Habits are routinized forms of action in which reflection is of minimal importance. Attitudes might be persistent preferences for certain ends, values, and forms of behavior. These all are formed by human experience in very complex ways; while critical reflection and judgment about them might change them, they are less subject to alteration than particular moral judgments might be, though they deeply condition both judgments and actions. What kinds of educational experience might affect these more persistent characteristics of moral selfhood?

4. Affective and emotive aspects of persons are important, for example, indignation with injustice. It is no doubt true that emotions are evoked by particular circumstances, persons, or events; a person may have a latent hostility toward tyranny, but his actual indignation is aroused only in the circumstances of actual unjust uses of power. There are differences in the emotions of different persons; some have a greater sense of indignation about injustice than others. And there are differences among persons in the extent to which they rely upon their emotions and sensibilities to determine their judgments and actions. Among moral philosophers, Max Scheler and Nicolai Hartmann both had a great deal of confidence in moral "feelings" for values. Hartmann could even write about "an astonishing infallibility" of the "order of the heart." [6] Just as affective life, as "sensibilities," are involved in discriminating responses to works of art, so they are involved in responses to human moral situations. What kinds of experiences or instruction make for refinement of affections, sensibilities, and emotions?

5. Motives and intentions have always been deemed to be important. Again we are faced with terms whose usage is subject to much discussion and dispute. For our purposes, these terms can be used to refer to "backward" and "forward" looking reasons for action, as they are commonly used in contemporary English moral philosophy (Anscombe and others). The question can be put in terms that are quite simple, as Nowell-Smith does: "For the sake of what does a man act?" The answers to this question will be many, and they raise the normative question of which reasons for action are morally more justifiable than others. The answers will vary in the extent of the generality of their reference also; in the same circumstances one person might say that he acts for the sake of the general welfare and another that he acts for the sake of preventing physical pain. There are general intentionalities which provide a basic direction for moral action but do not determine what one should do in every particular situation. What kinds of experience and education would be involved in the formation of motives and intentions that would meet with moral approval?

6. The capacity to make judgments is obviously involved. That men make moral judgments is a fact; how they make their judgments differs. Some are governed by stipulated traditional and institutionally authorized rules of conduct; others rely more upon intuitive responses. Some are governed by the strength of their emotions; others are more prepared to give rational accounts of their judgments. Can we teach better and worse ways to make moral judgments?

If what we have called moral selfhood includes at least these aspects, what is required in moral education depends upon what is most fitting to influence various ones of them. While moral education cannot be programmed so that parts of it will be related to aspects of moral selfhood, and so that it all will add up to the creation of morally responsible persons, it is clear that moral education, no matter under whose auspices it takes place, must be conceived in such a way that it does not ignore the complexity of persons who act.

VARIETIES OF MORAL EDUCATION

Hartmann wrote that "no one becomes good through instruction." [7] The sentence in itself is loaded with ambiguities, but his general point is clear enough and indicates at least a proper warning about expectations of the efficacy of education in morality. What was stated earlier must be remembered; even small children are already making moral judgments and are engaged in moral action. How persons are becoming the moral selves they will be is subject to various kinds of empirical research such as that conducted by Piaget, Kohlberg, and others. These studies can be used for clues as to how moral education might proceed. The failures of various kinds of moral education that have been attempted in the past could be rehearsed, for example, the memorization of moral beliefs and rules which have not necessarily altered moral conduct. What is offered here are observations and suggestions of an ethician who is not a specialist in educational techniques. Some of them are pertinent to various aspects of moral selfhood that have been outlined above.

First, it is possible in public schools and elsewhere to provide the occasions in which persons become critically aware of what is involved in making moral decisions and moral judgments. Social studies, for one example, are being taught at the junior high school and high school levels in such a way that students are required to make a judgment about the justice of some historical decision and defend the judgment that they make. Those skills in critical rational discourse that often in the past were confined to the debating team are being taught across the student body, thanks to new materials and teaching procedures coming from

Cambridge. Beginning with the judgments students do make about historical or contemporary situations, they can be helped to become aware not only of the factual matters needed to understand the circumstances but also of the moral values and principles by which they justify their decisions. They can be helped to analyze what they mean when they say that a decision or action is unjust, or unfair, or right or good. There is no way to guarantee that they will become morally "better" persons; indeed, professors of ethics who spend their professional lives dealing with such matters are not by virtue of that necessarily morally "better" men. But opportunities for critical analysis of moral decisions and actions, and of the arguments given in their defense can be provided, and thus greater sophistication can be developed in moral judgment-making on the part of students.

Second, some of the most profound and discriminating teaching of morality takes place through the study of drama, novels, poetry, biography and motion pictures. No doubt moral educators from Moses to the present have had, on the whole, a bias toward the highly generalized formulation of ethical principles and rules, or moral values. But moral actions are particular and concrete. Often the agenda of moral education has been set by the discrepancy between the generality of principles taught and the concreteness of particular deeds; we have had to show how general principles and rules can be applied to particular circumstances. This has been difficult for many reasons, not least of which has been the conflict that exists between certain general rules or between certain moral values. For example, persons might be taught to approve of both liberty and justice for various reasons; yet on particular occasions such as in proposed laws against racial discrimination in the rental of housing units, the conflicts between the abstractions become apparent as they are applied to the particular case. In contrast with this, drama, novels, poetry, biography, and motion pictures are often portrayals of particularities, and thus make vivid the nuances of emotions and sensibilities, of motives and intentions in moral experience.

Jesus, as a moral teacher, in continuity with a good rabbinical tradition, can be used to illustrate this point. He was arguing with a lawyer about a religious question that had a partially moral answer, "What shall I do to inherit eternal life?" They rehearsed the answers of the law, which included the requirement to love one's neighbor. Then the lawyer asked, "And who is my neighbor?" Jesus did not respond with a discourse on general principles and demonstrate how they could be applied to a concrete situation. Rather, he told a story, the widely remembered parable of the good Samaritan. The concreteness of the parabolic literary form has a cogency which more abstract discourse does not always have. It appeals to sensibilities as well as to intellect; it is nuanced and in some situations is eminently more effective for educational purposes than other modes of discourse.[8]

Certainly the morally and aesthetically sensitive teacher of the dramas of Sophocles and Shakespeare enables students to engage in moral reflection about motives and consequences, about sensibilities and emotions, about commitments and beliefs. Perhaps the aversion of a whole generation to "phoniness" and its prizing of honesty and integrity has been expressed by and informed by the widespread study of J. D. Salinger's *Catcher in the Rye*. The history teacher who is emancipated from textbooks that chronicle historical facts, and who uses case study materials, or biographies and autobiographies, can enable students to think morally as well as politically, militarily, economically, and socially about crucial decisions made by statesmen and by other citizens. Martin Luther King's *Stride Towards Freedom* portrays the concreteness and ambiguities of sensibilities and emotions, motives and intentions, beliefs and loyalties, character

and disposition in a way that no ethics textbook can, even
when it is sprinkled with illustrations and examples.

Third, action projects, whether under extracurricular
programs of public schools or under religious or other
auspices, can have a profound significance in the moral development of their participants. Aristotle reminded his
readers that to become a lyre player one has to practice playing the lyre; to become a courageous person (courage is a
moral virtue) one has to do courageous deeds. Not only moral
virtues can be developed from action projects; attitude
changes, awareness of the complexities of proposed actions,
determination of means appropriate to the ends sought,
sensitivity to both evil and good can be nurtured by new
occasions which demand decisions and actions. No doubt reflection on such experience is a required part of its use for
moral nurture; here in contrast with the use of dramas
and other writings the reflection can be based upon personal
experience.

Those persons who have a technical understanding of how
people learn and develop, and who have more imagination
than I, can, no doubt, conjure up more effective ways of
moral nurture. The most controversial issue for them in a
pluralistic society will be the normative matter of moral
beliefs, of commitments and loyalties to particular values and
ends, often embodied in particular communities and
persons. Which beliefs, which commitments and loyalties,
which values and ends are to be preferred? And why? In
free societies undergoing rapid change these questions will
always be answered differently by different persons and
groups, and the strains that this pluralism produces can
become severe. Neither novelty nor tradition is a sufficient
justification for moral beliefs. In the public forum of rational
discussion, and in the events in which persons acting from
radically different beliefs are in conflict, the examina-
tion of various aspects of morality necessarily goes on. It

might be necessary to develop some minimal consensus out of the conflict of beliefs, even though the consensus might be justified differently by different religious or other groups. At least, critical inquiry into all moral beliefs is necessary and valuable for the community as a whole; and certainly particular communities have the right to develop moral beliefs within such consensus as is necessary for just order in society, a consensus which is usually reflected in the public law.

Who is responsible for moral nurture? Certainly the family, the religious communities, the mass media, the public schools, and a host of voluntary associations. If moral nurture is thought of not in terms of packaged moral and spiritual values to be learned and sometimes applied but in terms of a continuous development of personal moral life, the dispersal of responsibility for it can be more readily understood. If morality is thought of as a dimension of human life and action, it cannot so readily be separated from our politics and economics, our literature and uses of science. There is no ready differentiation of function in our society which places responsibility for moral nurture exclusively on one institution or community. Respect for differences in belief and respect for moral autonomy ought not to deter public education, particularly from providing occasions in which persons can develop as responsible moral actors.

RELIGION AND MORAL EDUCATION

Our interest here is not so much in analyzing the division of labor between church and school as it is in stating briefly how religion *can* (not necessarily does) make some difference in a person's morality, and in his attitudes, decisions, and actions. Training in religious beliefs and attitudes is clearly the responsibility of the religious communities.

First, critical reflection about morality often leads to the question "Why be moral?" That is, men seek a justification for morality itself. Religions provide ways of justifying morality in general, as well as particular moral actions. This can be illustrated from the Bible. In the statements of the Ten Commandments in both Exodus 20 and Deuteronomy 5, there is a kind of "preamble" which is assumed to be the justification of the commandments themselves. "I am the Lord your God, who brought you out of the land of Egypt, out of the house of bondage" (Exodus 20:2, Deuteronomy 5:6). Because "I am the Lord your God," therefore "Thou shalt not kill," etc. Because I have done something liberating for you, in gratitude you ought to do the following sorts of things: not commit adultery, etc. Or, in the Christian letter to the Ephesians, the author writes, "Be sure of this, that no immoral or impure man, or one who is covetous (that is, an idolator) has any inheritance in the Kingdom of Christ and of God" (Ephesians 5:5). The reason for being moral is here a religious one; to have an inheritance in the Kingdom one must not be impure or immoral or covetous.

It is obvious that not all men who refrain from killing conform to that rule because "God is the Lord." It is just as obvious that many men in the history of the Christian community who seemed to want to inherit God's Kingdom were immoral, impure, and covetous. What is suggested here is that the connections between religious reasons for being moral and moral conduct itself are neither logically nor psychologically necessary. To refrain from immorality neither logically nor psychologically required belief in the Lordship of God, or the aspiration to inherit his Kingdom. Training in morality does not necessarily require training in religion.

Second, yet it is the case that believing (in a strong sense) certain things about God does, should, and ought to affect what I have called moral selfhood, and the moral actions of persons. This can be illustrated from a passage in the Bible, I John 4, which has love as its focus. A number of verses will be quoted, with remarks interspersed to show how religion and morality are related.

"Beloved, let us love one another." This commends a certain intention toward each other. "for love is of God." This makes God the author or source of this love; it authorizes the intention. "and he who loves is born of God and knows God." This is to claim that the person who loves is God's creature and is dependent upon him, and that by loving others he even knows or experiences God. "He who does not love does not know God; for God is love." This asserts in propositional form that God *is* love, and that therefore the person who does not act in love cannot know God. Through the congruity of the human act of love with what God is, one knows him. "In this is love, not that we loved God, but that he loved us and sent his Son to be the expiation for our sins." This is to affirm that man could not love God without God first having loved man, having done something to show that he loves man. "Beloved, if God so loved us, we also ought to love one another." If God loved, then we ought to love; a moral command is inferred from the statement of what God is and what God does. Man's moral life ought to be consistent with his beliefs about what God is and does. Man is to imitate God. "No man has ever seen God; if we love one another, God abides in us and his love is perfected in us." Here the astonishing claim is made that where men are loving, God is present.

The relationships between (a) God is love, (b) God loves us, (c) love is of God, (d) where men are loving God is present, (e) human love enables us to know God, (f) human love is "born of God," and (g) we ought to love one another, cannot be sorted out here. The modest intention is to show how religious faith and belief are claimed to affect moral dispositions, attitudes, and intentions, and to indicate how a moral imperative to love is inferred from a religious belief. Consistent with, or congruent with, belief in the proposition

"God is love" are loving attitudes, a disposition to be loving, a commandment to love, and even rules of conduct. But the relationship is not just one of congruence between religious propositions and moral statements. The relation of the religious man to God is one of confidence in him, of faithfulness to him; it is believing with passionate assent. This relationship, analogous to personal relationships with others, enables and requires certain moral beliefs, dispositions and attitudes, sensibilities, motives, and intentions.

What is the significance of these remarks for the conjunction between religion and moral nurture? These can be stated in brief form.

1. Moral training does not necessarily require religious training. There are other justifications for morality than religion; there are other experiences than religious ones which evoke commendable attitudes, intentions, and actions.

2. Religious training does not guarantee morally commendable conduct.

3. Religious training, trust, and belief have an intention distinct from moral education, namely, faith in, or orientation of life toward, God.

4. Religious training, trust, and belief have implications for morality. There are dispositions and attitudes, sensibilities, motives, and intentions which can be and ought to be evoked and nourished by religious life and faith. There are moral dispositions, motives, etc., that religious men ought to have if their actions are to be consonant, congruent, or consistent with their trust and beliefs.

Finally, religious moral training is not confined to authoritative rules of conduct and to sanctions of punishment and reward in eternity. It can and ought to, like other moral nurture, aid in developing autonomous, morally responsible persons. To quote from the Apostle Paul, "For you were called to freedom, brethren; only do not use your freedom as an opportunity for the flesh, but through love be servants of one another" (Galatians 5:13). And the same author wrote in a tract of religious and moral instruction, " 'All things are lawful,' but not all things are helpful. 'All things are lawful,' but not all things build up" (I Cor. 10:23).

CONCRETE PRINCIPLES AND THE RATIONAL
PASSIONS / *Richard S. Peters*

INTRODUCTION

In education content is crucial. There is some point in raising aloft the romantic banners of "development," "growth," and "discovery" when children are being bored or bullied. Romanticism is always valuable as a protest. But another sort of trouble starts when romantics themselves get into positions of authority and demand that children shall scamper around being "creative" and spontaneously "discovering" what it has taken civilized man centuries to understand. Some synthesis has to be worked out between established content and individual inventiveness. The basis for such a synthesis is to be found mainly in those public historically developed modes of experience whose immanent principles enable individuals to build up and revise an established content and to make something of themselves within it. In science, for instance, merely learning a lot of facts is a weariness of the spirit; but a Robinson Crusoe, untutored in a scientific tradition, could not ask a scientific question, let alone exhibit "creativity." Originality is possible only for those who have assimilated some content and mastered the mode of experience, with its immanent principles, by means of which this content has been established and repeatedly revised.

The same sort of Hegelian progression is detectable in morality. "Morality" to many still conjures up a "code" prohibiting things relating to sex, stealing, and selfishness. The very word "code" suggests a body of rules, perhaps of an arbitrary sort, that all hang together but that have no rational basis. To others, however, morality suggests much more individualistic and romantic notions, such as criterion-less choices, individual autonomy, and subjective preferences. Whether one experiences anguish in the attempt to be "authentic," produces one's commitment, like the white rabbit producing his watch from his waistcoat pocket, or proclaims, like Bertrand Russell, that one simply does not *like* the Nazis, the picture is roughly the same—that of the romantic protest. Synthesis must be sought by making explicit the mode of experience which has gradually enabled civilized people to distinguish what is a matter of morals from what is a matter of custom or law, and which has enabled them to revise and criticize the code in which they have been brought up, and gradually to stand on their own feet as autonomous moral beings. This they could never have done without a grasp of principles.

It is the details of this sort of synthesis that I propose to explore in this essay as a preliminary to discussing moral education; for it is no good talking about moral education until we have a more determinate conception of what is involved in being "moral." Because they are uncertain about this, many well-meaning parents and teachers are hamstrung in their attempts at moral education. If they incline toward the code conception, they tend to be authoritarian in their approach; if, on the other hand, they favor some variant of the romantic reaction, they may expect that children will go it alone and decide it all for themselves. A more adequate view of morality should reveal the proper place for both authority and self-directed learning in moral education. But I shall not have space to deal with details of such educational procedures in this essay—only to explore a middle road between these two extreme positions and to view the general contours of moral education from this vantagepoint.

THE FUNCTION OF PRINCIPLES

There are some, like Alasdair MacIntyre,[1] who seem to hold that we have no middle way between allegiance to a surviving code and some kind of romantic protest. For, it is argued, moral terms such as "good" and "duty," once had determinate application within a close-knit society with clear-cut purposes and well-defined roles; but now, because of social change, they have broken adrift from these concrete moorings. A pale substitute is left in generalized notions such as "happiness" instead of concrete goals, and duty for duty's sake instead of duties connected with role performances that were manifestly related to the goals of the community. So we have a kind of moral schizophrenia in the form of irresolvable conflicts between "interest" and "duty" and no determinate criteria for applying these general notions, because their natural home has passed away. It is no wonder, on this view, that those who have not been brought up in one of the surviving tribalisms make such a fuss about commitment and criterionless choice; for there is nothing else except those ancient realities to get a grip on.

The Emergence of a Rational Morality Based on Principles

But even if this is how concepts such as "good" and "duty" originated, why this nostalgic fixation on those stuffy, self-contained little communities, such as Sparta, where they could be unambiguously applied? Could not one be equally impressed by the Stoic concept of a citizen of the world, by the law of nations forged by the Roman jurisprudents, and by the labors of lawyers such as Grotius to hammer out laws of the sea against piracy? The point is that both science and a more rational, universalistic type of morality gradually emerged precisely because social change, economic expansion, and conquest led to a clash of codes and to conflict between competing views of the world. Men were led to reflect about which story about the world was true, which code was correct. In discussing and reflecting on these matters they came to accept higher order principles of a procedural sort for determining such questions.

MacIntyre, it is true, applauds those like Spinoza who drew attention to values connected with freedom and reason. He admits the supreme importance of truth-telling;[2] he notes the massive consensus about basic rules for social living first emphasized by the natural law theorists, which H. L. Hart has recently revived as the cornerstone of a moral system.[3] Why then is he so unimpressed by this consensus that he gives such a onesided presentation of the predicament of modern man? Mainly, so it seems, because an appeal to such principles and basic rules cannot give specific guidance to any individual who is perplexed about what he ought to do.

Difficulties About Concrete Guidance

Two connected difficulties are incorporated in this type of objection to principles. The first, already mentioned, is that no concrete guidance can be provided by them for an individual who wants to know what he ought to do. This is usually illustrated by the case of the young man who came to Sartre wanting guidance about whether he should stay at home and look after his aged mother or go abroad and join the Free French. How could an appeal to principles help him? Well, surely he only had a problem because he already acknowledged duties connected with his status as a son and as a citizen. Would Sartre have said to him "You have to decide this for yourself" if the alternative to joining the Free French had been presented as staying at home and accepting bribes from the Germans for information? And surely if what is claimed to be missing is a principle for deciding between these duties, there are principles which would rule out some reasons which he might give for pursuing one of the alternatives. Supposing, for instance, he said that he was inclined toward going abroad because he wanted to determine precisely the height of St. Paul's Cathedral. Would Sartre have applauded his exercise of criterionless choice?

The existentialist emphasis on "choice" is salutary, of course, in certain contexts. It is important, for instance, to stress man's general responsibility for the moral system which he accepts. This needs to be said against those who smugly assume that it is just there to be read off. It needs to be said, too, in the context of atrocities such as Belsen. It also emphasizes the extent to which character is destiny and the role which choices play in shaping the individual's character. In this kind of development, conflict situations are particularly important, and if fundamental principles conflict there is not much more that one can say than that the individual must make up his own mind or use his "judgment." But we do not decide on our fundamental principles such as avoiding pain or being fair; still less do we "choose" them. Indeed, I would feel very uneasy in dealing with a man who did. And why should a moral theory be judged by its capacity to enable the individual to answer the question "What ought I to do now?" as distinct from the question "What, in general, are there reasons for doing?" Do we expect casuistry from a moral philosopher or criteria for making up our own minds?

The more important difficulty is the one MacIntyre has in mind, that fundamental principles such as "fairness" or "considering people's interests" give us such abstract criteria that they are useless because they always have to be interpreted in terms of a concrete tradition. I am very sympathetic to this objection, but I think that it also applies in varying degrees to all rational activities. To take a parallel: all scientists accept some higher order principle such as that one ought to test competing hypotheses by comparing the deduced consequences with observations. But this does not give them concrete guidance for proceeding. It has to be interpreted. To start with, what is to count as an observation? The amount of social tradition and previous theory built into most observation procedures, especially in the social sciences, is obvious enough. And how is the importance of one set of observations to be assessed in relation to others? This is not unlike saying in the moral case: Consider impartially the suffering of people affected by a social practice. But what is to count as suffering and how is one person's suffering to be weighed against another's? But do difficulties of this sort render the procedural principles of science useless? If not, why should fundamental moral principles be regarded as useless?

Fundamental principles of morality such as fairness and the consideration of interests only give us general criteria of relevance for determining moral issues. They prescribe what sort of considerations are to count as reasons. Within such a framework men have to work out arrangements for organizing their lives together. And just as in science there is a fair degree of consensus at a low level of laws, so in the moral case there are basic rules, e.g., concerning contracts, property, and the care of the young, which any rational man can see to be necessary to any continuing form of social life, man being what he is and the conditions of life on earth being what they are. For, given that the consideration of interests is a fundamental principle of morality and given that there is room for a vast amount of disagreement about what, ultimately, a man's interests are, there are nevertheless certain general conditions which it is in any man's interest to preserve however idiosyncratic his view of his interests. These include not only the avoidance of pain and injury but also the minimal rules for living together of the type already mentioned. Above this basic level there is room for any amount of disagreement and development. People are too apt to conclude that just because some moral matters are controversial and variable, for instance sexual matters, the whole moral fabric is unstable. It is as if they reason: In Africa men have several wives, in Europe only one, in the U.S.A. only one at a time; therefore all morals are a matter of taste! As evils, murder and theft are just as culture-bound as spitting in the street!

The point surely is that stability and consensus at a basic level are quite compatible with change and experiment at other levels. Indeed to expect any final "solution," any secure resting place in social or personal life, is to be a victim of the basic illusion which is shared by most opponents of democracy, that of belief in some kind of certainty or perfection. But in determining what are basic rules and in seeking above this level ways of living which may be improvements on those we may have inherited, we make use of principles. Such principles have to be interpreted in terms of concrete traditions; they cannot prescribe precisely what we ought to do, but at least they rule out certain courses of action and sensitize us to features of a situation which are morally relevant. They function more as signposts than as guidebooks.

The Nature of Principles

A place for principles in the moral life must therefore be insisted on without making too far-flung claims for what they can prescribe without interpretation by means of a concrete tradition. Indeed I want to insist on the importance of such traditions for the learning of principles as well as for their interpretation. Before, however, this theme is developed in detail, more must be said about the nature of principles in order to remove widespread misunderstandings.

First of all, what are principles? A principle is that which makes a consideration relevant. Suppose that a man is wondering whether gambling is wrong and, in thinking about this, he takes account of the misery caused to the families of gamblers he has known. This shows that he accepts the principle of considering people's interests, for he is sensitized to the suffering caused by gambling rather than horror-struck at the amount of greenness in the world created by the demand for green tables. He does not, in other words, accept the principle of the minimization of greenness. He may or may not be able to formulate a principle explicitly. But this does not matter; for acceptance of a principle does not depend on the ability to formulate it and to defend it against criticism, as some, like Oakeshott,[4] who are allergic to principles, suggest. Rather it depends on whether a man is sensitized to some considerations and not to others.

Of course, formulation is necessary if one intends to embark on some moral philosophy in the attempt to justify principles. And it might well be said that the task of justifying them is a crucial one for anyone who is according them the importance I am according them. As, however, the central part of my *Ethics and Education*[5] was concerned with this very problem it would be otiose for me to present more than a thumbnail sketch of the arguments here. What I argued was that there are a limited number of principles which are fundamental but nonarbitrary in the sense that they are presuppositions of the form of discourse in which the question "What are there reasons for doing?" is asked seriously. The principles which have this sort of status are those of impartiality, the consideration of interests, freedom, respect for persons, and probably truth-telling. Such principles are of a procedural sort in that they do not tell us precisely what rules there should be in a society but lay down general guidance about the ways in which we should go about deciding such matters and indicate general criteria of relevance. It was argued that these principles are presuppositions of what is called the democratic way of life, which is based on the conviction that there is a better and a worse way of arranging our social life and that this should be determined by discussion rather than by arbitrary fiat.

Even if it is granted that arguments along these lines might be sustained for a few fundamental principles, further difficulties might still be raised. It might be said, for instance, that stress on the importance of principles in morality implies rigidity in the moral life. A picture is conjured up of Hardy-like characters dourly doing their duty whilst the heavens fall about them. Certainly some kind of firmness is suggested by the phrase "a man of principle." But here again, there are misunderstandings. A man of principle is one who is *consistent* in acting in the light of his sensitivity to aspects of a situation that are made morally relevant by a principle. But this does not preclude adaptability due to differences in situations, especially if there is more than one principle which makes different factors in a situation morally important.

Another time-honored objection is that principles are products of reason and hence inert. We may mouth them or assent to them, but this may be a substitute for acting in a morally appropriate way. Part of the answer to this objection is to be found in the answer to the criticism that links having principles with the ability to formulate them and to defend them. But there is a further point that needs to be made. Notions such as "fairness" and "the consideration of interests" are not affectively neutral. "That is unfair" is an appraisal which has more affinities with an appraisal such as "that is dangerous" than it has with a colorless judgment such as "that is oblong." Pointing out that someone is in pain is not at all like pointing out that he is 5 feet 6 inches tall.

The strength of the emotive theory of ethics derives from the fact that moral principles pick out features of situations which are not affectively neutral. This, however, does not make them inconsistent with living a life guided by reason; for this sort of life presupposes a whole constellation of such appraisals, e.g., that one should be consistent, impartial, and truthful, that one should have regard to relevance, accuracy, and clarity, and that one should respect evidence and other people as the source of arguments. It is only an irrationalist who welcomes contradictions in an argument, who laughs with delight when accused of inconsistency, or who is nonchalant when convicted of irrelevance. Science and any other rational activity presuppose such normative standards which are intimately connected with the passion for truth which gives point to rational activities. Unless people cared about relevance and had feelings about inconsistency science would not flourish as a form of human life. The usual contrast between reason and feeling is misconceived; for there are attitudes and appraisals which are the passionate side of the life of reason.

So much, then, for the usual objections to the conception of the moral life in which prominence is accorded to principles. I hope I have said enough to establish their place in it. I now want to show how they can be seen to function in relation to concrete traditions to which MacIntyre ascribes so much importance and how they can save us from the existentialist predicament which he views as the logical alternative to being encased in a surviving code.

THE COMPLEXITY AND CONCRETENESS
OF THE MORAL LIFE

A man who accepts principles is too often represented as
living in some kind of social vacuum and attempting to
deduce from his principles a concrete way of living. This is
an absurd suggestion. To start with, the disposition to appeal
to principles is not something that men have by nature, any
more than reason itself is some kind of inner gadget that
men switch on when the occasion arises. If thinking is the
soul's dialogue with itself, the dialogue within mirrors the
dialogue without. To be critical is to have kept critical
company, to have identified oneself with that segment of
society which accepts certain principles in considering its
practices. Rationality, of which science is a supreme example,
is itself a tradition. Rational men are brought up in the
tradition that traditions are not immune from criticism.

But criticism, thinking things out for oneself, and other
such activities connected with a rational type of morality,
cannot be exercised without some concrete content. For how
can one be critical without being brought up in something to
be critical of? How can one think things out for oneself unless
one's routines break down or one's roles conflict? Adherence
to principles must not be conceived of as self-contained; it
must be conceived of as being bound up with and modifying
some kind of content. Scientists cannot think scientifically
without having any content to think about.

Complexity

In an open society this content is considerably more
complex than in those small, self-contained communities
where, according to MacIntyre, concepts such as "good" and
"duty" had their natural home. The notion, for instance, that
people are persons with rights and duties distinct from those
connected with their roles is an alien notion in such close-knit
communities. But once this is admitted, as was widely the
case with the coming of Stoicism and Christianity, the content

of the moral life becomes immediately much more complicated. For the norms connected with treating people as persons begin to interpenetrate those connected with roles and with the accepted goals of life. In trying to get a clear idea, therefore, about the contours of our moral life it is necessary to consider its complexity before we can grasp the concrete ways in which principles enter into it. At least five facets of our moral life must be distinguished.

First of all, under concepts such as "good," "desirable," and "worthwhile," fall those activities which are thought to be so important that time must be spent on initiating children into them. These include things such as science, poetry, and engineering and possibly a variety of games and pastimes. Most of these are intimately connected not only with occupations and professions but also with possible vocations and ideals of life. In our type of society they provide a variety of options within which an individual can make something of himself if he is encouraged to pursue his own bent as the principle of freedom demands.

Second, under the concepts of "obligation" and "duty," fall ways of behaving connected with social roles. Much of a person's moral life is taken up with his station and its duties, with what is required of him as a husband, father, citizen, and member of a profession or occupation.

Third, there are those duties, more prominent in an open society, which are not specifically connected with any social role but which relate to the following of general rules governing conduct between members of a society. Rules such as those of unselfishness, fairness, and honesty are examples. These affect the manner in which an individual conducts himself within a role as well as in his noninstitutionalized relationships with others. They are personalized as character traits.

Fourth, there are equally wide-ranging goals of life which are personalized in the form of "motives." These are purposes not confined to particular activities or roles, which derive from non-neutral appraisals of a man's situation. Examples are ambition, envy, benevolence, and greed. An ambitious man, for instance, is one who is moved by the thought of getting ahead of others in a whole variety of contexts. Both traits of character and motives can be thought of as virtues and vices. The traits of fairness and honesty are virtues; those of meanness and selfishness are vices. The motives of benevolence and gratitude are virtues; those of greed and lust are vices. Both character traits and motives, when looked at in a justificatory context, incorporate considerations that can be regarded as fundamental principles. Examples would be fairness and benevolence, which can be appealed to in order to criticize or justify not only other traits and motives, but also conduct covered by activities and role performances.

There are, finally, very general traits of character[6] which relate not so much to the rules a man follows or to the purposes he pursues as to the manner in which he follows or pursues them. Examples would be integrity, persistence, determination, conscientiousness, and consistency. These are all connected with what used to be called "the will."

The point in spelling out this complexity of our moral life is to rid us straightaway of any simpleminded view that moral education is just a matter of getting children to have "good personal relationships" or to observe interpersonal rules like those relating to sex, stealing, and selfishness. It emphatically is not. To get a boy committed to some worthwhile activity, such as chemistry or engineering, is no less part of his moral education than damping down his selfishness; so also is getting him really committed to the duties defining his role as a husband or teacher. These duties, of course, must be interpreted in a way which is sensitized by the principle of respect for persons; but no adequate morality could be constituted purely out of free-floating personal obligations.[7]

Concreteness

So much for the complexity of the content of the moral life

which is to form the basis for any rational morality that appeals to principles. Let me now turn to the matter of concreteness in the interpretation of fundamental principles and moral ideals. The burden of the attack on principles by people like MacIntyre and Winch is to be found in Edmund Burke; it is that they are too abstract. "The lines of morality are not like the ideal lines of mathematics." My contention is that principles can be conceived of and must be conceived of as entering into the moral life in a perfectly concrete way without making them completely culture-bound.

Impartiality.[8] The most fundamental principle of all practical reasoning is that of impartiality. This is really the demand that excludes arbitrariness, which maintains that distinctions shall be made only where there are relevant differences. This is essential to reasoning, in that what is meant by a reason for doing A rather than B is some aspect under which it is viewed which makes it relevantly different. But though this principle gives negative guidance in that it rules out arbitrariness, making an exception of oneself, and so on, it is immediately obvious that it is quite impossible to apply without some other principle which determines criteria of relevance. The most obvious principle to supply such criteria is that of the consideration of interests, which is personalized in virtues such as benevolence and kindness.

The Consideration of Interests. In practice the rays of this principle are largely refracted through the prism of our social roles and general duties as members of a society. If we are teachers, for instance, considering people's interests amounts, to a large extent, to considering the interests of children entrusted to our care. I once taught with a man who had such a wide-ranging concern for people's interests that he used to tell his class to get on with some work and to sit there with them, writing letters to old scholars, in order to get them to subscribe to an "Aid to India" fund. His present scholars were, of course, bored to death! He certainly had a somewhat abstract approach to considering people's interests!

Most Utilitarians, following Mill and Sidgwick, have stressed the importance of Mill's "secondary principles" in morality. The Utilitarian, Mill argued, has not got to be constantly weighing the effects of his actions on people's interests any more than a Christian has to read through the Bible every time before he acts. The experience of a society with regard to the tendencies of actions in relation to people's interests lies behind its roles and general rules. The principle that one should consider people's interests acts also as an ever-present corrective to, and possible ground of criticism of, rules and social practices which can also be appealed to when rules conflict. This point is well made by Stephen Toulmin in his book on ethics.[9] A man could stick too closely to his role and accept too uncritically what was expected of him generally as a member of society. He might be very much an organization man or a man of puritanical disposition, riddled with rules that might have lost their point, or without sensitivity to the suffering caused by unthinking insistence on the letter of the law. What would be lacking would be that sensitivity to suffering caused by actions and social practices which finds expression in virtues such as benevolence, kindness, and what Hume called "the sentiment of humanity."

Freedom. Giving interpersonal support to the consideration of interests is the principle of freedom which lays it down that, other things being equal, people should be allowed to do what they want, or that, in other words, reasons should be given for constraining people in their pursuit of what they take to be good. This combines two notions, that of "wants" and that of "constraints," and immediately the concrete questions crowd in "What is it that people might want to do?" and "What sorts of constraints should be absent?" What, too, is to count as a constraint? Is it the want to walk about nude or to speak one's mind in public that is at issue? And are the constraints those of the bully or those of public opinion? The situation becomes even more complicated once we realize that, men being what they are, we are only in fact free from obnoxious constraints like those of the bully if we are willing to accept the milder and more leveling constraints of law. And so concreteness asserts itself. The principle only provides a general presumption, albeit one of far-reaching importance. At what point we decide that there are good reasons for constraining people because, for instance, they are damaging the interests of others, is a matter of judgment.

Closely related to the principle of freedom are ideals like "the self-development of the individual" and personal autonomy. But here again, concreteness is imperative, for what can "development" mean unless we build into the concept those modes of experience that it has taken the human race so long to evolve? And what sort of "self" is going to develop? Granted that this must come to a certain extent from the individual, who does this partly by his "choices," must not this "self" be fairly closely related to the normal stock of motives and character traits which are called virtues? And is it not desirable that higher order character traits, such as persistence and integrity, be exhibited in the development of this "self"? And how can the pressure for independence and the making of choices arise unless the individual genuinely feels conflicting obligations deriving from his occupancy of social roles and his acceptance of the general rules of a society? And what point is there in choice unless the individual thinks that what he decides can be better or worse, wise or foolish? And if he thinks that any particular act is not a pointless performance he must already accept that there are general principles which pick out relevant features of the alternatives open to him.

All of this adds up to the general conclusion that the ideals connected with the principle of freedom are unintelligible except against a background of desirable activities, roles, and rules between which the individual has to choose and that

any proper choice (as distinct from random plumping)
presupposes principles other than freedom in the light of
which alternatives can be assessed.

Respect for Persons. The same sort of point can be made
about respect for persons, another fundamental principle
which underlies and acts as a corrective to so many of our
formalized dealings with other men. Indeed, much of the
content of this principle has to be defined negatively in such
concrete contexts. To show lack of respect for a person is, for
instance, to treat him in a role situation as merely a
functionary, to be impervious to the fact that he, like us, has
aspirations that matter to him, is a center of evaluation and
choice, takes pride in his achievements, and has his own
unique point of view on the world. Or it is to treat him merely
as a participant in an activity who is to be assessed purely
in terms of his skill and competence in that activity. Worse
at something becomes generalized to worse as a human being.
In a similar way an excess of group loyalty or fellow-feeling
can make a man seem not just different in some respects but
generally inferior as a human being. Respect for persons, too,
is at the bottom of our conviction that some motives are
vices—lust, for instance, and envy and a certain kind of
humility.

So much, then, by way of a brief sketch to illustrate the
way in which I conceive of fundamental principles as entering
into the moral life in a manner perfectly consistent with its
complexity and concreteness. I now want to end by outlining
my conception of moral education, which goes with this
conception of the moral life.

MORAL EDUCATION

One or two general remarks must first be made about the
meaning of "education." There is a well-established generalized
use of "education" which refers, roughly, to any processes
of "rearing," "instruction," "training," etc., that go on at

home and at school. But there is a more specific sense of education which emerged in the nineteenth century in which education is distinguished from training and which is used to pick out processes that lead to the development of an "educated man." In this more specific sense, education involves getting people to make something of themselves within activities that are thought to be worthwhile, in a way which involves an understanding that has some kind of depth and breadth to it. In this more specific sense of education, employed by most educators when they are thinking about their tasks, all education is, therefore, moral education, if we are to include the pursuit of good in morals and not just confine it to codes and more general dealings with other men. Again, we will have to leave on one side the vexatious question of justification in the sphere of "the good," of why, in other words, chemistry is more worthwhile than baseball or sun-bathing. We can pursue the implications of this view of education without getting immersed in that issue, which is a veritable "Serbonian bog where armies whole have sunk." [10]

The first implication is that educating people has very much to do with getting them "on the inside" of what is worthwhile, so that they come to pursue and appreciate it for what there is in it as distinct from what they may conceive of is as leading on to. It is in relation to this criterion of education that I want to make sense of notions such as commitment and being authentic, which starkly confront the instrumental attitude of "What is the use of it?" and "Where is this going to get one?" I have sympathy for the philosopher who was pressed at an interview for a chair to commit himself to the view that philosophy must have some practical use— whatever that means. He exclaimed in exasperation, "Look, we may have to say that sort of thing in order to get money from governments and businessmen for universities, but for heaven's sake do not let us become victims of our own propaganda."

The second implication is that educating people must

involve knowledge and understanding. To be educated is not just to have mastered a know-how or knack, even if it is in the sphere of some very worthwhile activity such as cookery or ballet dancing. The Spartans were highly trained and skilled, but they are almost paradigms of a people who were not educated. Though depth of understanding is necessary to being educated, it is not sufficient, for a scientist can have a deep understanding of the "reasons why" of things and still be uneducated if all he understands is a specialized branch of science. "Education is of the whole man" is a conceptual truth in that being educated is inconsistent with being only partially developed in one's understanding—with seeing a car, for instance, as only a piece of machinery without aesthetic grace, without a history, and without potentialities for human good or ill. Let me now relate these two implications to the different facets of the moral life in order to show the indispensability of both content and principles and the proper place for the romantic ideal.

Commitment and Authenticity

One of the great enemies of education, in this specific sense, is second-handedness and instrumentality; hence Whitehead's polemic against inert ideas. What seems deplorable is not just that children should mug up some science because it is the done thing or in order to get good grades but that teachers should grind through their day with that dreadful fixed smile, or that people should be polite without sensing the point of it. Doing the done thing for conformity's sake seems a stifling corruption of the moral life, and, of course, it is an inherently unstable view; for a secondhand form of behavior is very susceptible to temptations and disintegrates when external pressures and incentives are withdrawn. This is tantamount to saying that moral education is centrally concerned with the development of certain types of motives, especially with what I have called the rational passions. When looked at in a justificatory context, some of these, e.g., benevolence, respect for persons, and the sense of justice, function as fundamental principles. But if such principles are to be operative in a person's conduct, they must become *his* principles. That means that they must come to function as motives, as considerations of a far-ranging sort that actually move him to act. Let us now consider the different facets of the moral life in the light of this commitment criterion of education.

Activities and Role-Performances. The trouble with the situation in which we are placed in education is not just that children do not always come to us glistening with a desire to learn what is worthwhile or with a predisposition toward mastering their duties; it is also that they are incapable of firsthand attitudes toward these activities and role performances until they are sufficiently on the inside of them to grasp them and be committed to what they involve. Although a child may have some degree of curiosity there is a great difference between this and the passion for truth which lies at the heart of an activity such as science, and until he feels strongly about this all-pervading principle that permeates science, it is difficult to see how his viewpoint can be anything but a bit external. He must, to a certain extent, be induced to go through the motions before he is in a position to grasp their point, and the point is given by the underlying principle, which personalizes one of the rational passions. To be rational is to care about truth; similarly, in the interpersonal sphere he must come to care about persons as centers of evaluation.

Of course there are all sorts of devices for bringing this about. In the old days, teachers, modeling the school on the army, used to employ a variety of coercive techniques. The progressives, in revolt, model the school more on the supermarket and try to gear their wares to children's wants and preferences. Then there are the less dramatic devices of stimulating by example and employing general guiding words such as "good" and "ought," which suggest that there are reasons but do not intimate clearly what the reasons are. The teacher's hope is that the proper reasons for doing things will become the pupil's actual reasons. This may come about by some process of identification. Admiration for a teacher may be turned outward toward involvement in the activities and forms of behavior to which he is committed, or an existing predisposition in the child, such as curiosity, may be gradually transformed by appropriate experience into the rational passion of respect for truth. This is likely to be greatly facilitated if the enthusiasm of the peer group is also enlisted, but this takes time and training. Let me illustrate this.

To be on the inside of an activity such as science or philosophy is not to have just a general curiosity or a merely abstract concern for truth. It is to be concretely concerned about whether particular points of view are true or false. These particularities are only intelligible within a continuing tradition of thought, which has been developed by people who adhere to a public stock of procedural principles. It is because of this concrete concern that they care desperately about things like the relevance of remarks, cogency in argument, and clarity of exposition; for how can one get to the bottom of anything without a concern about standards such as these which are indispensable to serious discussion? Sporadic curiosity is not enough; it has to be fanned into a steady flame and disciplined by adherence to the standards which regulate a common pursuit. The problem of education, as Whitehead saw only too well, is not just that of contriving the initial romance, it is that of bringing about acceptance of the precision and discipline required to wed a person to a pursuit. In this the support of the peer group is probably as important as the example and insistence of the teacher.

The judgment and skill which come with firsthand experience render activities more absorbing and worthwhile. The cultivation of personal relationships, for instance, and even sitting on committees, can become more and more absorbing as occupations for those who have a shrewd grasp of human behavior. Politics, as an activity, was quite different when practiced by Caesar rather than by Pompey, because

48

of the skill and understanding Caesar brought to it. Although it is satisfying sometimes to relapse into routine activities requiring little effort (a point, I think, which Dewey appreciated too little), and although there is something to be said for occasional incursions into simple, and sometimes more brutish forms of enjoyment, it would be intolerable for a rational man to spend most of his life in such a circumscribed way. A minimum task of moral education is surely to equip people so that they will not be perpetually bored. Therefore, the case for skill and understanding, on grounds purely of individual satisfaction, is a strong one. There is also the point that, as soon as knowledge enters in as an important ingredient in an activity, an additional dimension of value, deriving from the concern for truth, is opened up.

In a pluralistic society like ours there must be a high degree of consensus at the level of those fundamental principles which underlie democratic procedures and, as I have already argued, it is obvious enough that there must be agreement about a level of basic rules which provide conditions necessary for anyone to pursue his interests. But above this level there is bound to be controversy. In this sphere of "the good" or of personal ideals, with which we are at the moment concerned, there are any number of options open to individuals. And the principle of freedom demands that there should be. It is in this sphere that talk of commitment and authenticity is particularly pertinent. One man may develop a lifelong passion for science. Another, more influenced by the Christian ideal, may find that his main sphere of commitment is in the sphere of personal relationships and the relief of suffering. Another may opt for an aesthetic type of activity.

On the other hand, another person may find almost complete fulfillment in devoting himself to the fulfillment of a role, that of a teacher for instance. There has been a lot of loose talk, deriving from Sartre's celebrated example of the waiter, about the incompatibility of authenticity with occupying a role. Playing a role, which involves either simulation or second-handedness, should not be confused with a genuine commitment to a role. And, of course, as has been emphasized repeatedly, there is no role which can *completely* contain one's concerns and duties as a human being.

Interpersonal Rules. In the interpersonal sphere there may have to be firm insistence from the start on rules like those of keeping contracts, not stealing, punctuality, and honesty.[11] And why should children not *enjoy* mastering these rules as well as those of games? Unless, however, the reasons behind these rules eventually become the individual's reasons, the job is only half done. And this does not mean fostering a theoretical grasp of the conduciveness of such rules to the general good. That kind of notion never induced anyone to do anything except to preach theoretical revolution. Neither does it mean being swept by occasional gusts of sympathy when it dawns that somebody has suffered because he has been let down. It means, on the contrary, a steady but intense sensitivity to the consequences of actions, a constant and imaginative realization that in interpersonal relations one is dealing with persons who also have their unique point of view on the world and that this is something about them which matters supremely. In other words, it means the development of motives which personalize fundamental principles. It means also the development of judgment about particular moral matters that can only come to a person who has really got on the inside of this mode of experience. Making decisions and choices is too often represented as agonizing. For those who have attained some degree of wisdom it can be both a challenge and a delight.

It is not for a philosopher to pronounce on how children can be got on the inside of this more rational form of life, or on how the rational passions, which personalize fundamental principles, can best be awakened and developed. That is a matter for psychologists. The philosopher's role is only to indicate the sort of job that has to be done. But what he *can* say is that all talk of commitment and being authentic is vacuous unless this sort of job *is* done; for it is pointless to mouth these general injunctions unless concrete provision is made to implement them. What is to be lamented about young people today is not their lack of idealism but the difficulty of harnessing it to concrete tasks. Demonstrations, like mourning, are often symbolic expressions of feelings that have no obvious channel of discharge in appropriate action.

The Will. The importance of the rational passions can also be shown in the sphere of what used to be called "the will," where notions like those of integrity, determination, and resoluteness have their place. Of course this form of consistency is possible for people who adhere conscientiously to a simple code, perhaps because, like the colonel in *The Bridge over the River Kwai,* they accept unthinkingly some role-regulating principle such as "one ought always to obey orders" or "an officer must always care for his men." But such consistency is also possible for people with a more complicated morality if they genuinely care about the considerations which are incorporated in fundamental principles. Strength of character is so often represented in negative terms as saying no to temptation, as standing firm, as being impervious to social pressure. My guess is that rational people are able to do this only if they are passionately devoted to fairness, freedom, and the pursuit of truth and if they have a genuine respect for others and are intensely concerned if they suffer. As Spinoza put it: "Blessedness is not the reward of right living; it is the right living itself; nor should we rejoice in it because we restrain our desires, but, on the contrary, it is because we rejoice in it that we restrain them." [12] So much, then, for the first aspect of education, which concerns commitment to what is worthwhile. I now pass briefly to the second: that concerned with depth and breadth of understanding.

Depth and Breadth of Understanding

In any worthwhile activity or form of behavior there is a
mode of acting or thinking, with its underlying principles,
and some kind of established content which incorporates
the experience of those who are skilled in this sphere. Depth
is provided partly by the principles immanent in the mode
of experience and partly by the degree to which it has
been possible to discern the one in the many in the content.

The sin, of course, of the old formalism was to hand on
content in a secondhand way without encouraging children
to get on the inside of activities and to master the appropriate
mode of experience for themselves. The converse sin of the
progressive was to imagine that children could go it alone
without any proper grasp of content or of the underlying
mode of experience with its immanent principles. A more
modern sin is to assume that a mode of experience, or a
methodology, can be formalized and handed out and children
saved the trouble of mastering any content. Don't bother, it
is said, to teach children any historical facts, just teach them
to think historically. This reminds me of the yearning, which
one so often encounters, that one should hand out rules for
Clear Thinking in twelve easy lessons or that one should set
out philosophical method in advance of dealing with
particular philosophical arguments. Enough, I hope, has been
said about the intimate relationship between principles and
concrete content to avoid that particular rationalistic delusion.

In the interpersonal sphere of morality there is, of course,
a basic content, which every child must master, of rules to do
with noninjury, property, contracts, and so on; but
depth of understanding in this sphere is rather different. It is
not like depth of understanding in the sciences, which
consists in grasping more and more abstract theories; for
in morality one comes very quickly to nonarbitrary stopping
points in fundamental principles, such as the consideration
of interests. Depth consists rather in the development of the

imagination so that one can become more acutely aware of content to be given to these principles. What, for instance, is a man's interest? Above the level of physical and mental health what is to count? Surely not just what he thinks his interest to be? And so we start trying to understand various forms of worthwhile activity and personal ideals, not only in general but in relation to the capacity of particular individuals.

Respect for persons also opens up endless vistas for the imagination in making us vividly aware of the extent to which we drag our feet in failing to treat individuals and classes of people as persons in a full sense. It opens up, too, the whole realm of our understanding of persons. For understanding a person is more than being able to interpret his behavior in terms of wide-ranging psychological generalizations—even if there were any such generalizations that had been established—and it is not a mystic confrontation of "I" with "thou," about which there is little coherent that can be said. It is something about which a great deal can be said which is of cardinal importance for the moral life—about the way in which an individual's outlook is shaped by his roles, about his traits, and about his motives and aspirations. But most of this sort of knowledge we obtain by being with a person and sharing a common life with him, not by delving in psychological textbooks. This sort of knowledge is probably the most important sort for any moral agent to have; for our detailed appraisals of people are very closely intertwined with explanatory notions. Indeed, I made the point earlier that most motives and traits are also virtues or vices. And it may take a whole novel such as *Howards End* to explore concretely the range of an emotion like indignation.

Breadth of understanding, however, is of equal importance to depth in any concrete approach to the moral life. It has been argued that this life itself is a complex affair involving roles, activities, motives, and interpersonal rules. It also involves the disposition to be critical of this wideranging content in which any generation must necessarily be nurtured. The individual, too, may be confronted with conflicts arising from this heritage. How is he to be critical in an intelligent way about a social practice or about a particular feature of government policy unless he has some understanding of history and of the sorts of facts and unintended consequences of actions with which the social sciences are concerned? How is he to choose realistically between alternatives open to him unless he knows some facts?

It is absurd to encourage children to be critical and autonomous and not to insist on them learning facts which may inform their criticism and choices. In England, at the moment, we have all sorts of variants on the topic-centered curriculum, which is meant to induce moral commitment and to sensitize children to social issues. Discussion, of course, is the thing; it is regarded as almost sinful nowadays to instruct children in anything! But too often all that such discussions achieve is to confirm people's existing prejudices. They are not used as launching pads to dispatch children to the realm of some hard facts in the light of which they might make up their minds in an informed manner.

The same sort of point can be made about the necessity of breadth if children are to choose for themselves the sphere of activity within the wide range of what is desirable, to which they are to become personally committed and which may form the nucleus of a personal ideal. Not only must they have some breadth of content in order to be provided with concrete samples of the sorts of things between which they must choose; they must also make a concrete study of some of the forms of experience which have a special position in informing their choice. By this I mean studies such as literature, history, religion, and the social sciences, which, if imaginatively entered into, enlarge one's perspective of the predicament of man and so put one's own choice in a less abstract setting. The romantic ideal must at least have a classical background, if it is to function as more than a mere protest.

CONCLUSION

It might be said that my conception of moral education is indistinguishable from the ideal of a liberal education. I do not mind putting it this way provided that "liberal" implies no wishy-washiness and is used with awareness of the distinct emphases that it intimates.

A liberal education, to start with, is one that stresses the pursuit of what is worthwhile for what is intrinsic to it. It is hostile to a purely instrumental view of activities, to the bonds that link whatever is done to some palpable extrinsic end. The moral life, I have argued, rests upon rational passions which permeate a whole range of activities and which make them worthwhile for their own sake.

A liberal education is secondly one that is not narrowly confined to particular perspectives. I have argued both for a broad interpretation of the moral life and for the necessity of breadth of understanding to give concrete backing to the ideal of freedom, which is the most obvious ideal of liberalism.

Thirdly, a liberal education is one that is incompatible with authoritarianism and dogmatism. This is because a liberal education is based ultimately on respect for truth which depends on reasons and not on the word or will of any man, body, or book. This means, of course, not that there is not an important place for authority in social life, but that it has to be rationally justified—as indeed it can be in the bringing up of children. The use of authority must not be confused with authoritarianism. Respect for truth is intimately connected with fairness, and respect for persons, which, together with freedom, are fundamental principles which underlie our moral life and which are personalized in the form of the rational passions. The central purpose, however, of my essay, has been to show that adherence to such principles is a passionate business and that they can and should enter in a very concrete way into a man's activities, roles, and more personal dealings with other men.

EDUCATION FOR JUSTICE: A MODERN STATEMENT OF THE PLATONIC VIEW

Lawrence Kohlberg

When I called this essay a Platonic view I hoped it implied a paradox that was more than cute. It is surely a paradox that a modern psychologist should claim as his most relevant source not Freud, Skinner, or Piaget but the ancient believer in the ideal form of the good. Yet as I have tried to trace the stages of development of morality and to use these stages as the basis of a moral education program, I have realized more and more that its implication was the reassertion of the Platonic faith in the power of the rational good.

It is usually supposed that psychology contributes to moral education by telling us appropriate *methods* of moral teaching and learning. A Skinnerian will speak of proper schedules of reinforcement in moral learning, a Freudian will speak of the importance of the balance of parental love and firmness which will promote superego-identification, and so on. When Skinnerians or Freudians speak on the topic of moral education, then, they start by answering yes to Meno's question "Is virtue something that can be taught?" and go on to tell us how. In *Walden Two*, Skinner not only tells us that virtue comes by practice and reinforcement but designs an ideal republic which educates all of its children to be virtuous in this way.

My own response to these questions was more modest. When confronted by a group of parents who asked me "How can we help make our children virtuous?" I had to answer, as Socrates, "You must think I am very fortunate to know how virtue is acquired. The fact is that far from knowing whether it can be taught, I have no idea what virtue really is." Like most psychologists, I knew that science could teach me nothing as to what virtue is. Science could speak about causal relations, about the relations of means to ends, but it could not speak about ends or values themselves. If I could not define virtue or the ends of moral education, could I really offer advice as to the means by which virtue should be taught? Could it really be argued that the means for teaching obedience to authority are the same as the means for teaching freedom of moral opinion, that the means for teaching altruism are the same as the means for teaching competitive striving, that the making of a good storm trooper involves the same procedures as the making of a philosopher-king?

It appears, then, that we must either be totally silent about moral education or speak to the nature of virtue. In this essay, I shall throw away my graduate school wisdom about the distinction of fact and value and elaborate a view of the nature of virtue like that of Socrates and Plato. Let me summarize some of the elements of this Platonic view.

First, virtue is ultimately one, not many, and it is always the same ideal form regardless of climate or culture.

Second, the name of this ideal form is justice.

Third, not only is the good one, but virtue is knowledge of the good. He who knows the good chooses the good.

Fourth, the kind of knowledge of the good which is virtue is philosophical knowledge or intuition of the ideal form of the good, not correct opinion or acceptance of conventional beliefs.

Fifth, the good can then be taught, but its teachers must in a certain sense be philosopher-kings.

Sixth, the reason the good can be taught is because we know it all along dimly or at a low level and its teaching is more a calling out than an instruction.

Seventh, the reason we think the good cannot be taught is because the same good is known differently at different levels and direct instruction cannot take place across levels.

Eighth, then the teaching of virtue is the asking of questions and the pointing of the way, not the giving of answers. Moral education is the leading of men upward, not the putting into the mind of knowledge that was not there before.

I will spend little time on my disagreements with Plato, except to point out that I conceive justice as equality instead of Plato's hierarchy. I should note, however, that I have earlier discussed my views within John Dewey's framework.

In speaking of a Platonic view, I am not discarding my basic Deweyism, but I am challenging a brand of common sense first enunciated by Aristotle, with which Dewey partly agrees. According to Aristotle's *Ethics*, "virtue is of two kinds, intellectual and moral. While intellectual virtue owes its birth and growth to teaching, moral virtue comes about as a result of habit. The moral virtues we get by first exercising them; we become just by doing just acts, temperate by doing temperate acts, brave by doing brave acts."

Aristotle then is claiming that there are two spheres, the moral and the intellectual, and that learning by doing is the only real method in the moral sphere. Dewey, of course, does not distinguish the intellectual from the moral and objects to lists of virtues and vices in either area. Nevertheless, Deweyite thinking has lent itself to the Boy Scout approach to moral education which has dominated American practices in this field and which has its most direct affinities with Aristotle's views.

American educational psychology, like Aristotle, divides the personality up into cognitive abilities, passions or motives, and traits of character. Moral character, then, consists of a bag of virtues and vices. One of the earliest major American studies of moral character, that of Hartshorne and May, was conducted in the late twenties. Their bag of virtues included honesty, service, and self-control. A more recent major study by Havighurst and Taba added responsibility, friendliness, and moral courage to the Hartshorne and May bag. Aristotle's original bag included temperance, liberality, pride, good temper, truthfulness, and justice. The Boy Scout bag is well known, a Scout should be honest, loyal, reverent, clean, brave.

Given a bag of virtues, it is evident how we build character. Children should be exhorted to practice these virtues, should be told that happiness, fortune, and good repute will follow in their wake; adults around them should be living examples of these virtues; and children should be given daily opportunities to practice them. Daily chores will build responsibility; the opportunity to give to the Red Cross will build service or altruism, etc.

Let me quote a concrete program of moral education from Jonathan Kozol's book *Death at an Early Age. The Destruction of the Hearts and Minds of Negro Children in the Boston Public School*[1] Kozol says (pages 174-176):

> There is a booklet published by the Boston Public Schools bearing the title, "A Curriculum Guide in Character Education." This is the list of character traits which the teacher is encouraged to develop in a child: Obedience to duly constituted authority, self-control, responsibility, kindness, perseverance, loyalty, fair play.
>
> The section on obedience begins with the following selected memory gems. "We must do the thing we must before the thing we may; We are unfit for any trust til we can and do obey—Honor thy father and mother — True obedience is true liberty —The first law that ever God gave to man was a law of obedience."
>
> The section on self-control begins by the necessity for self-discipline by all people. The teacher is then advised to give examples of self-disciplined people, Abraham Lincoln, Charles Lindbergh, Robinson Crusoe, Florence Nightingale, Dwight D. Eisenhower.

It is hardly surprising that this approach to moral education doesn't work. Hartshorne and May found that participation in character education classes of this sort, in the Boy Scouts, in Sunday school did not lead to any improvement in moral character as measured by experimental tests of honesty, service, and self-control, and more recent research does not provide any more positive evidence as to the effects of character-building programs.

Let me point out, too, that while Kozol's example sounds both particularly systematic and particularly old fashioned, it is in principle pretty much that of enlightened public schools throughout the country. As long as teachers direct classroom groups, they must inevitably moralize about rules. They may choose to try to be value-neutral and treat all rules as traffic rules, that is, to assume that definition and maintenance of the rules is a matter of administrative convenience.

Let me cite an example from my observation of an enlightened and effective young fourth-grade teacher. The teacher was in the back of the room working with a project group, the rest of the class engaged with their workbooks. In the front row, a boy said something to his neighbor, who retaliated by quietly spitting in his face. The first boy equally quietly slugged the other without leaving his seat, by which time the teacher noted the disturbance. She said calmly, "Stop that and get back to your workbooks." The boy who had done the slugging said, "Teacher, I hit him because he spit in my face." The teacher replied, "That wasn't polite; it was rude. Now get back to work, you're supposed to be doing your workbooks." As they went back to work, the boy who had done the spitting said to his opponent with a grin, "I will grant you that; it was rude."

However, even teachers who prefer to keep moralizing oriented to traffic rules have to specify some moral goals. The teacher just mentioned had put together suggestions of the class in the form of a moral code, which was displayed in poster form at the back of the class. The code had the following commandments:

1. Be a good citizen
2. Be generous by helping our friends
3. Mind your own business
4. Work quietly
5. No fighting

6. Play nicely and fairly
7. Be neat and clean
8. Be prepared
9. Raise your hand
10. Be polite

While this code lacks a little in depth and completeness, a little more system and we would come up with one of the bags of virtues we have mentioned.

Let us try to systematize our objections to the bag of virtues, since it will start us on the road to a more Platonic view. Your reaction to the Boston program is likely to be similar to that of Kozol. He says (page 179), "You look in vain through this list for anything to do with an original child or an independent style, there is an emphasis on obedience characteristics. The whole concept of respect for unearned authority is bitter to children within these kinds of schools. I wonder whether anyone really thinks that you are going to teach character, or anything else by rattling off a list of all the people in America who have struggled to make good."

These comments don't themselves carry us very far, positively. They suggest a new bag of virtues centering on creativity instead of on obedience. They suggest substituting newer and more liberal models. Read Langston Hughes for Robinson Crusoe or Dwight Eisenhower.

Beyond a greater sympathy for the minds and hearts of Negro children, Kozol suggests no real solution. He does appear to suggest a solution in another setting, the Newton Junior High School described by him in a *New York Times Magazine* article (Oct. 29, 1967). There a modern moral education course is called "Man Alone" and is according to Kozol "a whirlwind tour of alienation, loneliness, dying and narcotics with writings from John Donne to Bruno Bettelheim." According to Kozol, in this class a picture of one of the Hell's Angels was projected on the wall in gory, swastika-painted vividness.

"Cool man, great," a voice shouted.

"That's sick," said another.

"He's honest anyway," chimed in another, "he's living out his own feelings."

"He's not faking."

Kozol goes on to say "the teacher then ventured the idea that an alienated person might not be able to be truly creative. A creative person is really alive and noncompulsive; alienation means the opposite."

In this seminar the class has turned the virtues around 180 degrees so that the Hell's Angels are truly honest and creative while the teacher uses psychological jargon about compulsivity and alienation to rotate the virtues back part way toward moral conformity. Clearly, this jazzing up of the bag of virtues has no more rational base than the program of the Boston public schools. There is no substitute for a good hard look at what virtue is.

Let us start at the beginning, then. The objection of the psychologist to the bag of virtues is that there are no such things. Virtues and vices are labels by which people award praise or blame to others, but the ways people use praise and blame toward others are not the ways in which they think when making moral decisions themselves. You or I may not find a Hell's Angel truly honest, but he may find himself so. Hartshorne and May found this out to their dismay forty years ago by their monumental experimental studies of children's cheating and stealing. In brief, they and others since have found:

1. You can't divide the world into honest and dishonest people. Almost everyone cheats some of the time; cheating is distributed in bell-curve fashion around a level of moderate cheating.

2. If a person cheats in one situation, it doesn't mean he will or won't in another. There is very little correlation between situational cheating tests. In other words, it is not a

character trait of dishonesty which makes a child cheat in a given situation. If it were, you could predict he would cheat in a second situation if he did in the first.

3. People's verbal moral values about honesty have nothing to do with how they act. People who cheat express as much or more moral disapproval of cheating as those who don't cheat.

The fact that there are no traits of character corresponding to the virtues and vices of conventional language should comfort us. Those who would try to capture for themselves the bag of virtues prescribed by the culture find themselves in the plight described by the theme song of the show, "You're a Good Man, Charlie Brown."

> You're a good man, Charlie Brown. You have humility, nobility and a sense of honor that is very rare indeed. You are kind to all the animals and every little bird. With a heart of gold, you believe what you're told, every single solitary word. You bravely face adversity; you're cheerful through the day; you're thoughtful, brave and courteous. You're a good man, Charlie Brown. You're a prince, and a prince could be a king. With a heart such as yours you could open any door—if only you weren't so wishy-washy.*

If, like Charlie Brown, we define our moral aims in terms of virtues and vices, we are defining them in terms of the praise and blame of others and are caught in the pull of being all things to all men and end up being wishy-washy. The attraction of the bag of virtues approach to moral education is that it encourages the assumption that everyone can be a moral educator. It assumes that any adult of

---

*Lyrics from the title song "You're a Good Man, Charlie Brown," from the musical play "You're a Good Man, Charlie Brown," words and music by Clark Gesner © 1965 and 1967 by Jeremy Music Inc. and reprinted by permission.

middle-class respectability or virtue knows what virtue is and is qualified to teach it by dint of being adult and respectable. We all have to make these assumptions as parents, but perhaps they are not sound. Socrates asked "whether good men have known how to hand on to someone else the goodness that was in themselves" and goes on to cite one virtuous Greek leader after another who had nonvirtuous sons. Shortly, I will describe what I believe to be a valid measure of moral maturity. When this measure was given to a group of middle-class men in their twenties and also to their fathers, we found almost no correlation between the two. The morally mature father was no more likely to have a morally mature son than was a father low on moral development. So numbers now support Socrates' bitter observation that good fathers don't have good sons or don't qualify as teachers of virtue.

In the context of the school, the foolishness of assuming that any teacher is qualified to be a moral educator becomes evident if we ask "Would this assumption make sense if we were to think of moral education as something carried on between one adult and another?" A good third-grade teacher of the new math and a good math teacher of graduate students operate under much the same set of assumptions. How many moralizing schoolteachers, however, would wish to make the claim that Protagoras made to young graduate students, that "I am rather better than anyone else at helping a man to acquire a good and noble character, worthy of the fee I charge."

If we think of moral education as something carried on at the adult level, we recognize that the effective moral educator is something of a revolutionary rather than an instiller of virtues. Protagoras could safely collect his fees for improving character because he meant by moral education the teaching of the rhetorical skills for getting ahead. When Socrates really engaged in adult moral education, however, he was brought up on trial for corrupting the Athenian youth.

Perhaps there is still nothing more dangerous than the serious teaching of virtue. Socrates was condemned to death, because, as he said in the *Apology:*

> I do nothing but go about persuading you all, old and young alike, not to take thought for your person or property, but for the improvement of the soul. I tell you virtue is not given by money, but that from virtue comes money, and every other good of man, public as well as private. This is my teaching, and if this is the doctrine which corrupts the youth, my doctrines are mischievous indeed. Therefore, Men of Athens, either acquit me or not; but whichever you do, understand that I shall never alter my ways not even if I have to die many times.

I stress the revolutionary nature of moral education partly because at this time it is comforting to reach back into history and recall that it is not only America that kills its moral educators. Martin Luther King joins a long list of men who had the arrogance not only to teach justice but to live it in such a way that other men felt uncomfortable about their own goodness, their own justice. In the last weeks, one has frequently heard the question, "Why King, not Carmichael or Brown?" It is not the man who preaches power and hate who gets assassinated. He is not a threat; he is like the worst in others. It is the man who is too good for other men to take, who questions the basis on which men erect their paltry sense of goodness, who dies.

Martin Luther King and Socrates as examples of moral educators suggest that while the bag of virtues encapsulated the need for moral improvement in the child, a genuine concern about the growth of justice in the child implies a similar concern for the growth of justice in the society. This is the implicit basis of Kozol's challenging the moral authority of a passive teacher in a ghetto school. I do not mean to imply by this that true moral education is a matter of political indoctrination of the young in the name of reform. Rather, I am arguing that the only constitutionally legitimate form of moral education in the schools is the teaching of justice and that the teaching of justice in the schools requires just schools. It has been argued by Ball[2] that the Supreme Court's Schemp decision calls for the restraint of public school efforts at moral education since such education is equivalent to the state propagation of religion, conceived as any articulated value system.

The problems as to the legitimacy of moral education in the public schools disappear, however, if the proper content of moral education is recognized to be the values of justice which themselves prohibit the imposition of beliefs of one group upon another. The requirement implied by the Bill of Rights that the schools recognize the equal rights of individuals in matters of belief or values does not mean that the schools are not to be "value-oriented." Recognition of equal rights does not imply value neutrality, i.e., the view that all value systems are equally sound. Because we respect the individual rights of members of particular groups in our society, it is sometimes believed that we must consider their values as valid as our own. Because we must respect the rights of an Eichmann, however, we need not treat his values as equal to that of the values of liberty and justice.

Public education is committed not only to maintenance of the rights of individuals but to the transmission of the values of respect for individual rights. The school is no more committed to value neutrality than is the government or the law. The school, like the government, is an institution with a basic function of maintaining and transmitting some, but not all, of the consensual values of society. The most funda-mental values of a society are termed moral, and the major moral values in our society are the values of justice. According to any interpretation of the Constitution, the rationale for government is the preservation of the rights of individuals, i.e., of justice. The public school is as much committed to the maintenance of justice as is the court. Desegregation of the schools is not only a passive recognition of the equal rights of citizens to access to a public facility, like a swimming pool, but an active recognition of the responsibility of the school for "moral education," i.e., for transmission of the values of justice on which our society is founded. From our point of view, then, moral education may legitimately involve certain elements of social reform if they bear directly on the central values of justice on which the public schools are based.

The delicate balance between social reform and moral education is clarified by the example of Martin Luther King if you recognize that King was a moral leader, a moral educator of adults, not because he was a spokesman for the welfare of the Negroes, not because he was against violence, not because he was a minister of religion, but because, as he said, he was a drum major for justice. His words and deeds were primarily designed to induce America to respond to racial problems in terms of a sense of justice, and any particular action he took had value for this reason and not just because of the concrete political end it might achieve.

I have used King as an example of a moral educator to indicate that the difference between the political reformer and the moral educator is not a difference in the content of their concern. Civil rights is as much a matter of morality as is honesty in financial matters. The distinctive feature of moral education as against ordinary political action is in the relation of means and ends. A black power politician using unjust means in the name of civil rights is clearly not in the enterprise of teaching justice anymore than is the policeman in the enterprise of teaching honesty when he shoots down rioters. In King's case, however, acts of civil disobedience flowed directly from a sense of principles of justice and thus were moral leadership, not just propaganda or protest.

Let me recapitulate our argument so far. We have

criticized the bag of virtues concept of moral education on the grounds first that there were no such things and second, if they were, they couldn't be taught or at least we didn't know how or who could teach them. Like Socrates, we claimed that ordinary people certainly didn't know how to do it, and yet there were no expert teachers of virtue as there were for the other arts. Rather than turning to nihilism, we pointed to an effective example of a moral educator at the adult social level, Martin Luther King. Since we could not define moral virtue at the individual level we tried it at the social level and found it to be justice and claimed that the central moral value of the school, like that of the society, was justice. Justice in turn is a matter of equal and universal human rights. We pointed to the cloud of virtue-labels attributed to King and pointed out that only one meant anything. Justice was not just one more fine-sounding word in a eulogy, it was the essence of King's moral leadership.

My hope is to have stirred some feelings about the seriousness and the reality of that big word, that Platonic form, justice, because men like King were willing to die for it. I suppose there may have been men willing to die for honesty, responsibility, and the rest of the bag of virtues, but, if so, we have no empathy with them. I am going to argue now, like Plato, that virtue is not many, but one, and its name is justice. Let me point out first that justice is not a character trait in the usual sense. You cannot make up behavior tests of justice, as Hartshorne and May did for honesty, service, and self-control. One cannot conceive of a little set of behavior tests that would indicate that Martin Luther King or Socrates were high on a trait of justice. The reason for this is that justice is not a concrete rule of action, such as lies behind virtues like honesty.

To be honest means don't cheat, don't steal, don't lie. Justice is not a rule or a set of rules, it is a moral principle. By a moral principle we mean a mode of choosing which is universal, a rule of choosing which we want all people to

adopt always in all situations. We know it is all right to be
dishonest and steal to save a life because it is just, because
a man's right to life comes before another man's right to
property. We know it is sometimes right to kill, because it
is sometimes just. The Germans who tried to kill Hitler
were doing right because respect for the equal values of
lives demands that we kill someone murdering others in order
to save their lives. There are exceptions to rules, then, but
no exception to principles. A moral obligation is an obligation
to respect the right or claim of another person. A moral
principle is a principle for resolving competing claims, you
versus me, you versus a third person. There is only one
principled basis for resolving claims: justice or equality.
Treat every man's claim impartially regardless of the man. A
moral principle is not only a rule of action but a reason for
action. As a reason for action, justice is called respect for
persons.

Because morally mature men are governed by the principle
of justice rather than by a set of rules, there are not many
moral virtues but one. Let us restate the argument in Plato's
terms. Plato's argument is that what makes a virtuous action
virtuous is that it is guided by knowledge of the good. A
courageous action based on ignorance of danger is not
courageous; a just act based on ignorance of justice is not
just, etc. If virtuous action is action based on knowledge of
the good, then virtue is one, because knowledge of the good
is one. We have already claimed that knowledge of the good
is one because the good is justice. Let me briefly document
these lofty claims by some lowly research findings. Using
hypothetical moral situations, we have interviewed children
and adults about right and wrong in the United States, Britain,
Turkey, Taiwan, and Yucatan. In all cultures we find the
same forms of moral thinking. There are six forms of thinking
and they constitute an invariant sequence of stages in each
culture. These stages are summarized in the table.

Levels and Stages in Moral Development

Levels	Basis of Moral Judgment	Stages of Development
I	Moral value resides in external, quasi-physical happenings, in bad acts, or in quasi-physical needs rather than in persons and standards	*Stage 1:* Obedience and punishment orientation. Egocentric deference to superior power or prestige, or a trouble-avoiding set. Objective responsibility
		Stage 2: Naively egoistic orientation. Right action is that instrumentally satisfying the self's needs and occasionally others'. Awareness of relativism of value to each actor's needs and perspective. Naive egalitarianism and orientation to exchange and reciprocity
II	Moral value resides in performing good or right roles, in maintaining the conventional order and the expectancies of others	*Stage 3:* Good-boy orientation. Orientation to approval and to pleasing and helping others. Conformity to stereotypical images of majority or natural role behavior, and judgment by intentions
		Stage 4: Authority and social-order maintaining orientation. Orientation to "doing duty" and to showing respect for authority and maintaining the given social order for its own sake. Regard for earned expectations of others

Levels and Stages in Moral Development, *continued*

Levels	Basis of Moral Judgment	Stages of Development
III	Moral value resides in conformity by the self to shared or shareable standards, rights, or duties	*Stage 5:* Contractual legalistic orientation. Recognition of an arbitrary element or starting point in rules or expectations for the sake of agreement. Duty defined in terms of contract, general avoidance of violation of the will or rights of others, and majority will and welfare
		Stage 6: Conscience or principle orientation. Orientation not only to actually ordained social rules but to principles of choice involving appeal to logical universality and consistency. Orientation to conscience as a directing agent and to mutual respect and trust

Why do I say existence of culturally universal stages means that knowledge of the good is one? First, because it implies that concepts of the good are culturally universal. Second, because an individual at a given level is pretty much the same in his thinking regardless of the situation he is presented with and regardless of the particular aspect of morality being tapped. There is a general factor of maturity of moral judgment much like the general factor of intelligence in cognitive tasks. If he knows one aspect of the good at a certain level, he knows other aspects of the good at that level. Third, because at each stage there is a single principle of the good, which only approaches a moral principle at the higher levels. At all levels, for instance, there is some reason for regard for law and some reason for regard for rights. Only at the highest stage, however, is regard for law a regard for universal moral law and regard for rights a regard for universal human rights. At this point, both regard for law and regard for human rights are grounded on a clear criterion of justice which was present in confused and obscure form at earlier stages.

Let me describe the stages in terms of the civil disobedience issue in a way that may clarify the argument I have just made. Here's a question we have asked: Before the Civil War, we had laws that allowed slavery. According to the law if a slave escaped, he had to be returned to his owner like a runaway horse. Some people who didn't believe in slavery disobeyed the law and hid the runaway slaves and helped them to escape. Were they doing right or wrong?

A bright, middle-class boy, Johnny, answers the question this way when he is ten: "They were doing wrong because the slave ran away himself. They're being just like slaves themselves trying to keep 'em away." He is asked, "Is slavery right or wrong?" He answers, "Some wrong, but servants aren't so bad because they don't do all that heavy work."

Johnny's response is Stage 1: *Punishment and obedience orientation.* Breaking the law makes it wrong; indeed the badness of being a slave washes off on his rescuer.

Three years later he is asked the same question. His answer is mainly a Stage 2 *instrumental relativism.* He says: "They would help them escape because they were all against slavery. The South was for slavery because they had big plantations and the North was against it because they had big factories and they needed people to work and they'd pay. So the Northerners would think it was right but the Southerners wouldn't."

So early comes Marxist relativism. He goes on: "If a person is against slavery and maybe likes the slave or maybe dislikes the owner, it's OK for him to break the law if he likes, provided he doesn't get caught. If the slaves were in misery and one was a friend he'd do it. It would probably be right if it was someone you really loved."

At the end, his orientation to sympathy and love indicates the same Stage 3, *orientation to approval, affection, and helpfulness* better suggested by Charlie Brown.

At age nineteen, in college, Johnny is Stage 4: *Orientation to maintaining a social order of rules and rights.* He says: "They were right in my point of view. I hate the actual aspect of slavery, the imprisonment of one man ruling over another. They drive them too hard and they don't get anything in return. It's not right to disobey the law, no. Laws are made by the people. But you might do it because you feel it's wrong. If 50,000 people break the law, can you put them all in jail? Can 50,000 people be wrong?"

Johnny here is oriented to the rightness and wrongness of slavery itself and of obedience to law. He doesn't see the wrongness of slavery in terms of equal human rights but in terms of an unfair economic relation, working hard and getting nothing in return. The same view of rights in terms of getting what you worked for leads Johnny to say about school integration: "A lot of colored people are now just living off of civil rights. You only get education as far as you want to learn, as far as you work for it, not being placed with someone else, you don't get it from someone else."

Johnny illustrates for us the distinction between virtue as the development of principles of justice and virtue as being unprejudiced. In one sense Johnny's development has involved increased recognition of the fellow-humanness of the slaves. From thinking of slaves as inferior and bad at age ten he thinks of them as having some sort of rights at age nineteen. He is still not just, however, because his only notions of right are that you should get what you earn, a conception easily used to justify a segregated society. In spite of a high school and college education, he has no real grasp of the conceptions of rights underlying the Constitution or the Supreme Court decisions involved. Johnny's lack of virtue is not that he doesn't want to associate with Negroes, it is that he is not capable of being a participating citizen of our society because he does not understand the principles on which our society is based. His failure to understand these principles cuts both ways. Not only does he fail to ground the rights of Negroes on principles but he fails to ground respect for law on this base. Respect for law is respect for the majority. But if 50,000 people break the law, can 50,000 be wrong? Whether the 50,000 people are breaking the law in the name of rights or of the Ku Klux Klan makes no difference in this line of thought.

It is to be hoped that Johnny may reach our next stage, Stage 5, *social contract legalism,* by his mid-twenties, since some of our subjects continue to develop up until this time. Instead of taking one of our research subjects, however, let us take some statements by Socrates as an example of Stage 5. Socrates is explaining to Crito why he refuses to save his life by taking advantage of the escape arrangements Crito has made:

> Ought one to fulfill all one's agreements?, Socrates asks. Then consider the consequences. Suppose the laws and constitution of Athens were to confront us and ask, Socrates, can you deny that by this act you intend, so far as you have power, to destroy us. Do you imagine that a city can continue to exist if the legal judgments which are pronounced by it are nullified and destroyed by private persons? At an earlier time, you made a noble show of indifference to the possibility of dying. Now you show no respect for your earlier professions and no regard for us, the laws, trying to run away in spite of the contracts by which you agreed to live as a member of our state. Are we not speaking the truth when we say that you have undertaken in deed, if not in word, to live your life as a citizen in obedience to us? It is a fact, then,

that you are breaking covenants made with us under
no compulsion or misunderstanding. You had seventy
years in which you could have left the country if you
were not satisfied with us or felt that the agreements
were unfair.[3]

As an example of Stage 6, *orientation to universal moral
principles,* let me cite Martin Luther King's letter from a
Birmingham jail.

There is a type of constructive non-violent tension
which is necessary for growth. Just as Socrates felt it
was necessary to create a tension in the mind so that
individuals could rise from the bondage of half-truths,
so must we see the need for nonviolent gadflies to
create the kind of tension in society that will help
men rise from the dark depths of prejudice and
racism.
One may well ask, "How can you advocate breaking
some laws and obeying others?" The answer lies in
the fact that there are two types of laws, just and
unjust. One has not only a legal but a moral responsibility to obey just laws. One has a moral responsibility
to disobey unjust laws. An unjust law is a
human law that is not rooted in eternal law and
natural law. Any law that uplifts human personality
is just, any law that degrades human personality is
unjust. An unjust law is a code that a numerical or
power majority group compels a minority group to
obey but does not make binding on itself. This is
difference made legal.
I do not advocate evading or defying the law as would
the rabid segregationist. That would lead to anarchy.
One who breaks an unjust law must do so openly,
lovingly, and with a willingness to accept the penalty.
An individual who breaks a law that conscience tells
him is unjust, and willingly accepts the penalty of

imprisonment in order to arouse the conscience of the community over its injustice, is in reality expressing the highest respect for law.

King makes it clear that moral disobedience of the law must spring from the same root as moral obedience to law, out of respect for justice. We respect the law because it is based on rights, both in the sense that the law is designed to protect the rights of all and because the law is made by the principle of equal political rights. If civil disobedience is to be Stage 6, it must recognize the contractual respect for law of Stage 5, even to accepting imprisonment. That is why Stage 5 is a way of thinking about the laws which are imposed upon all, while a morality of justice which claims to judge the law can never be anything but a free, personal ideal. It must accept the idea of being put in jail by its enemies, not of putting its enemies in jail. While we classified Socrates' statements to Crito as Stage 5, his statement of his civilly disobedient role as a moral educator quoted earlier was Stage 6, at least in spirit.

Both logic and empirical study indicate there is no shortcut to autonomous morality, no Stage 6 without a previous Stage 5.

We have claimed that knowledge of the moral good is one. We now will try to show that virtue in action is knowledge of the good, as Plato claimed. We have already said that knowledge of the good in terms of what Plato calls opinion or conventional belief is not virtue. An individual may believe that cheating is very bad but that does not predict that he will resist cheating in real life. Espousal of unprejudiced attitudes toward Negroes does not predict action to assure civil rights in an atmosphere where others have some prejudice; however, true knowledge, knowledge of principles of justice, does predict virtuous action. With regard to cheating, the essential elements of justice are understood by both our Stage 5 and our Stage 6 subjects. In cheating, the critical issue is recognition of the element of contract and agreement implicit in the situation, and the recognition that while it doesn't seem so bad if one person cheats, what holds for all must hold for one. In a recent study, 100 sixth-grade children were given experimental cheating tests and our moral judgment interview. The majority of the children were below the principled level in moral judgment; they were at our first four moral stages. Seventy-five percent of these children cheated. In contrast, only 20 percent of the principled subjects, that is, Stage 5 or 6, cheated. In another study conducted at the college level, only 11 percent of the principled subjects cheated, in contrast to 42 percent of the students at lower levels of moral judgment. In the case of cheating, justice and the expectations of conventional authority both dictate the same behavior. What happens when justice and authority are opposed?

An experimental study by Stanley Milgram[4] involved such an opposition. Under the guise of a learning experiment, undergraduate subjects were ordered by an experimenter to administer increasingly more severe electric shock punishment to a stooge victim. In this case, the principles of justice involved in the Stage 5 social contract orientation do not clearly prescribe a decision. The victim had voluntarily agreed to participate in the experiment, and the subject himself had contractually committed himself to perform the experiment. Only Stage 6 thinking clearly defined the situation as one in which the experimenter did not have the moral right to ask them to inflict pain on another person. Accordingly, 75 percent of those at Stage 6 quit or refused to shock the victim, as compared to only 13 percent of all the subjects at lower stages.

A study of Berkeley students carries the issue into political civil disobedience. Berkeley students were faced with a decision to sit in the Administration building in the name of political freedom of communication. Haan and Smith administered moral judgment interviews to over 200 of these students.[5] The situation was like that in Milgram's study. A Stage 5 social contract interpretation of justice, which was that held by the University administration, could take the position that a student who came to Berkeley came with foreknowledge of the rules and could go elsewhere if he did not like them. About 50 percent of the Stage 5 subjects sat in. For Stage 6 students, the issue was clear cut, and 80 percent of them sat in. For students at the conventional levels, Stages 3 and 4, the issue was also clear cut, and only 10 percent of them sat in. These results will sound very heartwarming to those who have engaged in protest activities. Protesting is a sure sign of being at the most mature moral level; however, there was another group who was almost as disposed to sit in as the Stage 6 students. These were our Stage 2 instrumental relativists, of whom about 60 percent sat in. From our longitudinal studies, we know that most Stage 2 college students are in a state of confusion. In high school most were at the conventional level, and in college they kick conventional morality, searching for their thing, for self-chosen values, but cannot tell an autonomous morality of justice from one of egoistic relativism, exchange, and revenge. Our longitudinal studies indicate that all of our middle-class Stage 2 college students grow out of it to become principled adults. If the pressures are greater and you are a Stokely Carmichael, things may take a different course.

I make the point to indicate that protest activities, like other acts, are neither virtuous nor vicious, it is only the knowledge of the good which lies behind them which can give them virtue. As an example, I would take it that a Stage 6 sense of justice would have been rather unlikely to find the Dow Chemical sit-in virtuous. The rules being disobeyed by the protesters were not unjust rules, and the sit-in was depriving individuals of rights, not trying to protect individual rights. Principled civil disobedience is not illegitimate propaganda for worthy political causes, it is the just questioning of injustice.

I hope this last example will indicate the complexity of the behaviors by which knowledge of justice may be manifested and that no trait of virtue in the ordinary sense will describe the behavior of the principled or just man. Having, I hope, shown the validity of the Platonic view of virtue, I will take the little time left to consider the sense in which it may be taught. The Platonic view implies that, in a sense, knowledge of the good is always within but needs to be drawn out like geometric knowledge in Meno's slave. In a series of experimental studies, we have found that children and adolescents rank as "best" the highest level of moral reasoning they can comprehend. Children comprehend all lower stages than their own, and often comprehend the stage one higher than their own and occasionally two stages higher, though they cannot actively express these higher stages of thought. If they comprehend the stage one higher than their own, they tend to prefer it to their own. This fact is basic to moral leadership in our society. While the majority of adults in American society are at a conventional level, Stages 3 and 4, leadership in our society has usually been expressed at the level of Stages 5 and 6, as our example of Martin Luther King suggests. While it may be felt as dangerous, the moral leadership of the Platonic philosopher-ruler is nonetheless naturally felt.

Returning to the teaching of virtue as a drawing out, the child's preference for the next level of thought shows that it is greeted as already familiar, that it is felt to be a more adequate expression of that already within, of that latent in the child's own thought. If the child were responding to fine words and external prestige he would not pick the next stage continuous with his own, but something else.

Let me now suggest a different example in the sense in which moral teaching must be a drawing out of that already within. At the age of four my son joined the pacifist and vegetarian movement and refused to eat meat, because as he said, "it's bad to kill animals." In spite of lengthy Hawk argumentation by his parents about the difference between justified and unjustified killing, he remained a vegetarian for six months. Like most Doves, however, his principles recognized occasions of just or legitimate killing. One night I read to him a book of Eskimo life involving a seal-killing expedition. He got angry during the story and said, "You know, there is one kind of meat I would eat, Eskimo meat. It's bad to kill animals so it's all right to eat Eskimos."

For reasons I won't detail, this eye for an eye, tooth for a tooth concept of justice is Stage 1. You will recognize, however, that it is a very genuine though four-year-old sense of justice and that it contains within it the Stage 6 sense of justice in shadowy form. The problem is to draw the child's perceptions of justice from the shadows of the cave step by step toward the light of justice as an ideal form. This last example indicates another Platonic truth, which is that the child who turns from the dark images of the cave toward the light is at first still convinced that his dark images best represent the truth. Like Meno's slave, the child is initially quite confident of his moral knowledge, of the rationality and efficacy of his moral principles. The notion that the child feels ignorant and is eager to absorb the wisdom of adult authority in the moral domain is one which any teacher or parent will know is nonsense. Let me give another example. Following a developmental timetable, my son moved to an expedient Stage 2 orientation when he was six. He told me at that time, "You know the reason people don't steal is because they're afraid of the police. If there were no police around everyone would steal." Of course I told him that I and most people didn't steal because we thought it wrong, because we wouldn't want other people to take things from us, and so on. My son's reply was, "I just don't see it, it's sort of crazy not to steal if there are no police."

The story indicates, that like most ordinary fathers, I had no great skill in teaching true virtue. My son, of course, has always been virtuous in the conventional sense. Even when he saw no rational reason for being honest, he received the highest marks on his report card on the basis of the bag of virtues of obedience, responsibility, and respect for property. Contrary to what we usually think, it is quite easy to teach conventionally virtuous behavior but very difficult to teach true knowledge of the good.

The first step in teaching virtue, then, is the Socratic step of creating dissatisfaction in the student about his present knowledge of the good. This we do experimentally by exposing the student to moral conflict situations for which his principles have no ready solution. Second, we expose him to disagreement and argument about these situations with his peers. Our Platonic view holds that if we inspire cognitive conflict in the student and point the way to the next step up the divided line, he will tend to see things previously invisible to him.

In practice, then, our experimental efforts at moral education have involved getting students at one level, say Stage 2, to argue with those at the next level, say Stage 3. The teacher would support and clarify the Stage 3 arguments. Then he would pit the Stage 3 students against the Stage 4 students on a new dilemma. Initial results with this method with a junior high school group indicated that 50 percent of the students moved up one stage and 10 percent moved up two stages. In comparison, only 10 percent of a control group moved up one stage in the four-month period involved.[6]

Obviously, the small procedures I have described are only a way station to genuine moral education. As my earlier comments suggested, a more complete approach implies full student participation in a school in which justice is a living matter. Let me sketch out one Platonic republic with this aim, a boarding school I recently visited.[7] The heart of this school is described in its brochure somewhat as follows:

> The sense of community is most strongly felt in the weekly Meeting, consisting of faculty, their families

and students. Decisions are made by consensus rather than by majority rule. This places responsibility on each member to struggle to see through his own desires to the higher needs of others and the community, while witnessing the deepest concerns of his conscience. The results of these decisions are not rules in the traditional sense, but agreements entered into by everyone and recorded as minutes.

The brochure goes on to quote a letter by one of its graduating students:

The School is an entity surrounded by the rest of the world in which each individual struggles against that which restrains him—himself. It has been said that the School gives too much freedom to its young, often rebellious students. But a film will darken to a useless mass of chemical if it's not developed in time. People change early, too. If they meet a loving atmosphere, they are affected by it profoundly. Growing up is a lonely thing to be doing, but at the Meeting School, it is also a beautiful thing.

All schools need not and cannot be self-contained little Republics in which knowledge of the good is to be brought out through love and community as well as through participation in a just institution. Such schools do stand as a challenge to an educational establishment which makes a pious bow to the bag of virtues while teaching that true goodness is tested on the College Boards. The Platonic view I've been espousing suggests something still revolutionary and frightening to me if not to you, that the schools would be radically different places if they took seriously the teaching of real knowledge of the good.

MORAL EDUCATION / *Bruno Bettelheim*

Dean Sizer, in planning this series of lectures on moral education, spoke of the conviction nowadays that recent changes in our families, churches, and communities are forcing the schools more and more to take on the moral education of the young. He wondered if this is really the case, and if so, how the schools could achieve it. But being a wise man, he also wondered if we might not be asking the wrong questions.

Let me begin by asserting what seems obvious to me: that of course neither the home, nor the churches, nor the communities have stopped teaching morality for a moment. What has happened during the last half century or so is that some of this teaching has become confusing, contradictory, uncertain. Also, its contents have become very different from what an unexamined popular voice still calls the moral virtues. One result is that children nowadays are exposed to a teaching of widely divergent values, compared to a still recent era when those taught by home, church, community, and school were one and the same.

More important, while the morality taught by home, church, and community (up to roughly the start of World War II) gave direct support to the school in its efforts to teach the young in traditional ways, this is no longer so in all cases. On the contrary, the morality now taught to many children before they come to school, and while there, is often largely at variance with the school's educational efforts.

Compare yesterday's conviction that the purpose of all human activity is to gain us eternal salvation with the conviction of many, today, that life is a rat race. Or compare the once accurate conviction that unless most of us work long and hard hours, and are thrifty, we and our children will starve, with the present conviction that economic hardships are unnecessary and that everyone is entitled to a guaranteed income. To state my problem baldly: Here is an educational system resting on a morality which holds that if man is to survive in this world it is absolutely necessary for him to acquire a certain sum of knowledge and skills. But how is the educator to reach a person who is convinced that society owes him a living no matter what—either because of past injustices inflicted on him or because our modern technology makes that easily possible?

Now what are some of these modern views of morality which, though not always openly stated or understood as such, still pervade much of after-school life and sometimes the life in the classroom? Let me cite only two quite significant prophets of modernity. According to Nietzsche, "fear is the mother of morality" and "morality is the rationalization of self-interest."

Certainly the psychoanalyst agrees with Nietzsche that morality is nourished by fear and that, in the final analysis, the content of morality is self-interest. After all, it is self-interest that makes one wish for eternal salvation, just as it is self-interest that makes one wish to succeed in the rat race. Where these types of self-interest differ is that the first leads to entirely different behavior from the second.

But as for morality being based on fear, nowadays we want to remove fear from the life of the child. And as for the content of morality, we often insist that it should not be self-interest. In short, we want the child to obey a morality whose fundamental motives we do our best to remove.

Now while Nietzsche's are at least absolute statements, Darwin, the second of my prophets, stressed how relative morality is and how it arises from the particular conditions one grows up with. Thus "if men were reared under precisely the same conditions as hive-bees, there can hardly be a doubt that our unmarried females would, like the worker bees, think it a sacred duty to kill their brothers; and mothers would strive to kill their fertile daughters."

What is wrong in all this is that each of the statements just quoted is an absolute, even the absolute statement about the relativity of morals. They are perhaps not wrong in themselves, but for all the practical purposes of education they are too limited to be valid, because, when applied to our problem, they neglect to account for developmental psychology, especially its model of a slowly developing ego. So long as morals were viewed as god-given, immutable, absolute, this did not matter. Morality could then be the same for young children and fully grown adults. So long as the only book worth reading was the Good Book, it was read alike by all ages. Only as an infinite variety entered our literature did the ability to understand and appreciate it become a matter of age grading. That is, one can live successfully and learn well in school as long as one's growing up begins with a very firm and stringent morality of absolutes, based on fear. Later, in the process of gaining maturity, one can slowly free oneself of some of the fear and begin to question its absolute tenets.

It was a Darwin, as well as a Nietzsche and a Freud— raised for so much of their lives on a stringent and absolute morality based on fear—who could later afford to question it ever more critically, but without ever losing too much of it to go to pieces as persons or to withdraw from the world in disgust. It was precisely the absolute morality instilled in them as children which made them strong enough, later on in life, to try to reshape the world by their now more mature moral concepts.

The mistake is that today too many believe that what ripe maturity can contain is therefore the best fare for immaturity. The mistake we still make is to hope that more and more citizens will have developed a mature morality, one they have critically tested against experience, without first having been subject as children to a stringent morality based on fear and trembling. Essentially everything I shall say from here on is nothing but an elaboration of this notion.

In the recent controversy about whether our schools serve

the underprivileged well, it has been pointed out again and again that current methods and procedures, including our teaching materials, are geared to the middle-class child. Thus Professor Moynihan, in discussing the Coleman report, asks "Can a middle class school be created without a middle class student body?" "I believe," he continues, that "Coleman's answer would have to be a highly tentative 'maybe'." [1]

I would like to go beyond Moynihan and assert that no school with the goals of our present educational system can achieve them well unless it has first instilled in its students what we might call a middle-class morality, because none of the learning it expects of its students can take place without it.

What is this "middle-class morality"? Essentially it consists of the conviction that to postpone immediate pleasure in order to gain more lasting satisfactions in the future is the most effective way to reach one's goals. It is this morality alone that makes learning possible, whether in communistic countries or in our own.

Now unfortunately for education, the modern views of morality cited earlier do not prepare the young to act on the basis of long-range goals. It takes mature judgment to be able to "do the right thing" when one is no longer motivated by fear and to do it though one knows how relative all human values are. The reason is that conscience (or the superego) is formed at a very early age and is, after all, largely irrational. On the basis of fear (not of reasoned judgment) it tells the child what he must do and must not do. Only later does the mature ego apply reason to these do's and don'ts and subject these earliest laws slowly, step by step, to a critical judgment.

Thus, while conscience develops on the basis of fear, learning depends on the prior formation of a conscience, which, in the process of learning, is more and more modified by reason. It is true that too much fear interferes with learning, but for a long time learning does not proceed well unless also motivated by some fear. And this is true until such time as self-interest is enlightened enough so that it alone is sufficient motive to power learning all by itself. But such is rarely the case before late adolescence, when personality formation is essentially completed.

This means that the small child who is taught to think (or whose life experience teaches him) that taking things without permission is all right on some occasions but not on others will have a superego that is full of holes, one that will not later support him toward academic achievement. Kant's categorical imperative requires a maturity of judgment, an ability to step outside one's private world and appreciate the experience of others, which is not available to the young. The meager experience that forms the world of the young does not permit such objectivity. To the immature mind the sometimes yes and sometimes no means only that I can act as I please.

A more refined morality must have as its base a once rigid belief in right and wrong based on a fear of perdition that permits of no shading, of no relativity. And when I speak here of perdition, it makes no difference whether perdition amounts to damnation in hell or the loss of parental affection. If, as modern middle-class parents are often advised, affection is guaranteed to the child no matter what, there will be no fear. But neither will there be much morality.

This means that diligence, concentration, and perseverance do not come about because of self-interest alone, as we seem to want to believe, but because of an irrational, superego anxiety. Only when this has grown habitual, become an inseparable part of the personality, is the anxiety no longer necessary for learning. Witness the fact that our under-privileged children who realize full well that it would be ego correct to learn well in school, since they wish to gain better jobs, cannot do so. The reason is that in the arduous task of learning, their ego is not sufficiently powered by instinctual energy. And the ego is not invested with such energy because these children are lacking in the most basic experience of physical and emotional well-being. But only these satisfactions will lead to libidinal investment of the ego because of its tested value in assuring them ample results.

Or to put it differently: All education is based on a middle-class morality that finds its psychoanalytic equivalent in a powerfully developed reality principle which insists that one must largely forego present pleasure for greater gains in the future. The trouble is that this, too, is not learned on a rational basis, but through anxiety instilled by the parents and by their example. If parents do not live by a stringent morality and by the reality principle, neither will their children.

But the poor no longer fear perdition if they do not always walk the narrow path of virtue, and the reality principle does not seem to work to their advantage; hence they are not likely to present their children with an image of stringent morality or of a stringent adherence to the reality principle. The result is that their children cannot internalize parental morality to form the content of a superego, nor later of an ego, and hence do not have these to live by. But, without them, they operate for the rest of their lives on a primitive ego which is always a pleasure ego. They prefer the experience that gives immediate pleasure.

Those who live by the pleasure principle can therefore make good use of an educational experience if it is made enjoyable to them. But they remain essentially uneducable and uneducated, though they may acquire bits of knowledge and skills, because the experience of pleasure, even around intellectual matters, does not change the pleasure principle into the reality principle.

If this is so, and if many of our children no longer acquire an absolute morality in the home and community, cannot function by the reality principle, then our problem is to use education to so reorganize the child's inner world, his personality, that he learns these things in school.

Freud seemed to believe, and so do I, that this can only be done if the teacher first recognizes the necessary conditions for learning and, second, acquires a true understanding of the slow-developing ego, including how and why morality is learned. It means above all that education cannot proceed without taking due account of the pupil's state of ego development and what the teacher may infer about his development from his social origins. If we wish to educate the child, as opposed to trying to pound some information into him—which is almost useless, since knowledge cannot thus be acquired—we must know where he comes from, who he is, and where he wishes to go; that is, we must first understand his moral existence.

That such knowledge on the part of the teacher is absolutely necessary if she is to educate the child often goes unrecognized, because for a sizable part of our school population the moral makeup of student and teacher is (or was) identical. Where this is so, all goes so smoothly that we overlook not only the differences but also how they account for failures in the system. These differences, where they do exist, make education impossible, but if they are not even recognized they cannot become the basis of educational planning and procedures.

The neglect of such discrepancies is what bedevils so many of our attempts to educate the underprivileged. We resort to half measures because we do not recognize the Janus-like character of education: That it must reach the child as the person he presently is, in order to guide him to where he is not. While most educators recognize the second of these goals, they seem reluctant to meet the first. But without the first, as Dewey knew and Pestalozzi knew before him, the second goal will never be achieved.

Our textbook writers, for example, were finally forced to

recognize that if stories about nice, white, blond, blue-eyed middle-class children are good material for teaching reading to nice, white, blond, blue-eyed middle-class children, that does not make them good readers for underprivileged Negro children. But the much-vaunted new readers for Negro children still steer away from large areas of Negro reality in both their illustrations and their text. No kinky hair in these pages, no Negroid facial features. They do not show or tell about living in overcrowded homes, of not knowing who one's father is, of having to live by gang rule. In pictures they tell of nice Negro children enjoying the corner drugstore, not trying to pilfer from it. And if they did depict reality as it is for the underprivileged Negro child, I doubt it would further his education, because, while recognizing where he is, it fails to guide him to where his development should take him.

Even if teachers like Kohl[2] or Ashton-Warner[3] begin where the child is socially, racially, and emotionally and look also toward where the child is going, it is still not enough, though it is very much a step in the right direction, because there is too little concern with the vehicles that alone can take the child there.

Let's look at how Ashton-Warner taught her Maori children, who are perhaps even more excluded from their New Zealand society than are our underprivileged Negro children. In her novel *The Spinster,* her heroine is a teacher who realized that these children wrote exciting stories of their own. The titles of their stories were less apt to be "Fun with Dick and Jane" than "I'm Scared." So one of them, when encouraged to write her own story, wrote: "I ran away from my mother, and I hid away from my mother. I hid in the shed and I went home and got a hiding." And a six-year-old wrote: "Mummie said to Daddy give me that money else I will give you a hiding. Daddy swear to Mummie. Daddy gave the money to Mummie. We had a party. My father drank all the beer by himself. He was drunk."

A comparison of these stories, with their matter-of-fact acquaintance with strong emotions about the life that proceeds in their homes, with those told in our own up-to-date primers, suggests why Ashton-Warner's Maori children learned well with her: because she recognized that an appeal to the emotions can succeed where an appeal to the intellect fails; that we must indeed start where the child is.

And so did Kohl and many like him. Only in the long run it worked as poorly for the Maori children as for Kohl's culturally deprived children in New York. With a few rare exceptions they enjoyed learning what they enjoyed learning, and when they no longer enjoyed it, they stopped learning. What these inspired teachers overlooked—and inspired teachers they were—is that nowhere will the vast majority of teachers be inspired and inspiring, that an educational system resting only on what the inspiring teacher can do must end in failure. And if anyone thinks that changing the system will enable us to supply all our slum schools with inspired teachers, then he banks on the millenium instead of planning for reality.

Such thinking rests on an image of the teacher as a perfect human being, an image that was not too different in the recent past when teachers were expected neither to drink nor to smoke or have sex. Yesterday's educational system required perfection of its teachers; we wanted no real live human beings to teach, but angels from heaven. True, what constitutes perfection has radically changed. We no longer expect the ideal teacher to be the puritanical virtues incarnate. We merely expect her to embody another set of virtues, ones that are only present in the rarest of persons—and even they seem unable to live such a rarified existence for more than a few years of their lives. To base our educational planning on perfect teaching and teachers is to cheat the overwhelming majority of all children who of necessity will have to be taught by average teachers.

Actually these exceptional teachers knew, but did not give

its rightful place, the fact that much of learning is not just
a pleasurable experience but hard work. And there is no
easy transition from pleasure to hard work. If one has
learned to enjoy both, then one can combine them. If not,
one can do only the first and not also the second. Or to
restate my earlier point: We do not reach ego achievements
because of id motivation alone. On the basis of id motivation
we master only what in some fashion pertains to the id. The
voice of reason is very soft. It is easily drowned out by the
voice of our appetites. If our teaching is based on pleasing
the emotions, the noisy clamor of emotions will drown out
the quiet voice of reason any day of the week.

How then do we learn? We learn best when the ego is
well functioning, that is, when it serves id, superego, and
the demands of reality all at once and when it is supported
in its learning tasks by stringent demands from the superego.
Whenever these conditions are not met there is ego weakness
and conflict. And such conflict, where not resolved (as by
sublimation, etc.), detracts from the ability to learn or makes
it frankly impossible.

Nor can the ego support learning when the demands of the
id overwhelm us because they are not satisfied. An empty
stomach that clamors for food, a rotting tooth that hurts, a
body abused by lack of rest, a mind that worries what
violence awaits him on the streets or at home, all these will
swamp the ego as immediate pressures and prevent learning,
because an ego overwhelmed by an unsatisfied id is much
too weak to succeed in its work. It means there must be not
only a strong superego but a fairly satisfied id for the
average boy or girl to enjoy the fairly balanced state of ego
(or mind) that alone permits learning in class. (The unusual
ones we need not worry about, since they will almost always
learn no matter what).

Now this superego, as suggested earlier, is unreasonably
domineering at first and says "you must do as you're told"

and not "sometimes yes and sometimes no." Then in the slow process of learning and maturation it says more and more "I must do what will be best for me in the long run." I think what is wrong with the education of so many children today is that they suffer from both: an ego that is weakened by the onslaught of unsatisfied instinctual desires and a poorly established superego. And the superego may be just as weakened by lack of content as by our wishing that from its very inception it would already be what it can only become after years of applying reason to unreasoned fears. What was wrong with old-fashioned education was that it disregarded the need to modify the superego in a continuous process, so that the motivating power of irrational anxiety would steadily give way to more rational purpose.

As a matter of fact, one primary motive for learning is precisely the wish to modify an irrationally demanding superego to make it more reasonable. If there is no striving for this, because there is no excessive superego anxiety to reduce, a most important motive for learning is absent. If we do not fear God, why learn about religion? If we do not fear the forces of nature, why learn about them? The detachment that permits hard study out of sheer curiosity, out of a desire to know more, is a stance arrived at only in full maturity.

imp. motive for learning = superego anxiety

?

Lacking a very strong superego we can still learn, on the basis of our emotions, what for one reason or another we want to learn, but we can learn only that. Such learning can and does take place on the basis of the pleasure principle. That is why educators who try to reach their students this way are amazed at how fast and how much their children learn. It is also why they quit in disappointment when everything breaks down as soon as learning can no longer proceed on the basis of the pleasure principle only. All other learning (which means most of it) can occur only when we have learned to function on the basis of the reality principle, because learning that gives no immediate pleasure satisfaction requires that we function by the reality principle, that is, are well able to accept displeasure at the moment, and for some time to come, in the hope of gaining greater satisfaction at a much later time.

Now with modern education, this later time becomes very late indeed, perhaps some fifteen years later. And the more we tax the reality principle, that is, the longer we postpone the satisfaction we strive for, the more likely it is to give way, in which case the pleasure principle becomes dominant again, unless the superego is much more powerful than it now is for most of our children. That explains why the longer the period of schooling, the greater the rate of dropouts—even for our nice, middle-class children, even for students at our best colleges—and the more apt they will be to seek the easy way out that drugs seem to offer.

Here, let's not forget that fifteen years (up to fairly recently) was half the span of a man's life. To be able to put off reaping the harvest for such a span needs a powerful domination of the pleasure principle by the reality principle, and the longer the span of time spent on education, the more dominant the reality principle must be for any learning to take place. This, in practical terms, is what teachers mean when they speak of the need for discipline, attention, and concentration.

Fortunately for education as it now exists, most middle-class children still enter school with a very strong superego and the reality principle dominant, with the ability to postpone pleasure over long stretches of time well established. Because this is so, we can still believe that our system works and that all the children fed into it do profit. Indeed it still works, but percentage-wise for fewer and fewer; and their number is constantly declining. Partly this is because the time spent on education has so increased, but more importantly it is because we live no longer in a scarcity economy but in theoretical affluence. Scarcity, at least in modern Western society, makes the reality principle seem to be the only way of life that assures survival. But the image of the affluent society plays havoc with the puritanical virtues.

If one's entire life is swept up in the idea of working now for rewards in the hereafter, then postponement of pleasure is in the very nature of things. When a child's primer begins, as did the first primer on this continent, printed in 1727, with the lines: "In Adam's fall, we sinned all. Thy life to mend, this book attend," then indeed we have set the stage correctly for an education that is based on a reality principle powered by the most stringent of superego anxieties, for an almost indefinite postponement of results to be worked for all the days of our life on this earth.

Whoever has made his own the conviction of sin expressed in the first sentence of the primer, as they formed the essence of life for all children who then went to school, is well prepared to devote all his energies to the educational task mapped out in the second: the injunction to attend to this book. He knows that only education, as here conceived, will save him from eternal hell. On the basis of such a superego anxiety he will apply himself well to education. But even then such an overweening ascendance of the reality principle had to be supported by the immense pleasure one expected to gain for such a tremendous postponement: Nothing less than the glories of heaven made it possible to wait that long for satisfaction, as only the terrors of hell could power such an overweening superego.

We no longer put store in such beliefs and no longer can or want to base academic learning on fear. We know how crippling a price of inhibition and rigidity it exacts. But the child must fear something if he is to apply himself to the arduous task of learning. My contention is that for education to proceed children must have learned to fear something before they come to school. If it is not the once crippling fear

fear necessary

of damnation and the woodshed, then in our more
enlightened days it is at least the fear of losing parental love
(or later, by proxy, the teacher's) and eventually the fear
of losing self-respect.

Here again the trouble is the old one: In order to fear the
loss of self-respect one must first have acquired it. (And as
the child grows older, this should be the major fear spurring
all actions, including academic learning.) But self-respect and
its demands are merely what have taken the place of older
and irrational superego demands. If those were never
established, then nothing else can take their place. Self-respect
is also the heir of an earlier and even deeper respect for the
parent (because he reliably protects us from pain and want).
If there has been no such respect for the parent, no self-respect
can take its place. On this too we reach the same circle:
A parent who is not deeply respected will not evoke much
fear about the loss of his love. Hence it might be said to
the modern parent that if he no longer wants to base his
child's superego on fear, then he must make doubly sure
that he is most highly respected. (And the same goes again
for the teacher who will later stand in *loco parentis*).
Otherwise, respect for him will not lead the child to identify
with him and his high standards of behavior till they
become the high standards of his own behavior.

What *do* we do, then, for those children whose behavior in
school shows they have not changed yet, or not significantly
so, from the pleasure to the reality principle? Sometimes we
start them even sooner on a learning they have no use for
and which hence falls flat; or we try to teach them on the basis
of the pleasure principle—as far as such learning can go—
or on what little of the reality principle they have made their
own. Only neither learning goes very far, though some
achievements will seem startling at the moment.

Obviously, realistic teaching, including that of morality,
would require us to assess the degree to which a child

coming to school has made the reality principle his own. If he has not done so sufficiently, then all educational efforts must be geared toward helping him accept it as more valid than the pleasure principle, helping him to make it his own, to internalize it. This can be done, though it is difficult, and it becomes the more difficult, the older the child.

How to do it is a lengthy and complex story. As a minimum I should say that our ability to postpone must be based on the repeated experience that it pays off in the future. The injunction not to grab and eat a cookie right now will only be effective if the child gets a great deal of praise and affection for the postponement, if his hunger has always been satiated pleasantly and fully in the past, and because he fears that by grabbing he will be losing the source of all this very certain satisfaction. No praise will work with the hunger unstilled, no demand be effective without the conviction that postponement will achieve greater gains (i.e., satiation and praise) and will certainly lead to no loss, whereas eating right now will lead to satiation, but only with anxiety and guilt. No postponement is possible, if all my experience tells me that "what I don't grab now I'll never get."

That is why it is so often observed that the underprivileged child can learn only as long as the teacher's attention is focused on him, if he at least gets rewarded by emotional closeness at the moment of trying to achieve. Too much of his life has consisted of the experience that if he doesn't grab it now, be it attention, praise, or other rewards, he won't get it later on. This is another reason why an education that takes so many years to produce results (jobs, money) is unable to reach children who do not believe that future rewards can result from energy spent now. For example, in my efforts to teach teachers this seemingly simple principle I was nearly always up against their puritanical ethic, according to which waste is sinful, that is, will be punished by scarcity in the future. This adherence to an inflexible reality principle has scrvcd thcm wcll, has enabled them to make it through college and become teachers. It is their own past experience that makes them believe in it so strongly. What they have long ago forgotten is that their present ways are the consequences of how early their adherence to the pleasure principle proved ineffective, compared to the very substantial gains they achieved by adapting to the reality principle.

But these children whom the teacher is now teaching merely grab when she distributes clean paper or pencils or maps and (in the teacher's eyes) waste all their supplies. Let me present here a kind of composite picture, from actual tapes, of what teachers say when I try to discuss this problem with them: "The children who are culturally deprived in my room have a tendency to waste the paper much more than other children in the class. Sometimes such a child will start to do something on a piece of paper. But if it's not up to his own standard, or what he thinks is my standard, he'll throw it away, or say 'this is no good' and ball it up. Then he wants another piece of paper. He can't think of turning the paper over. He won't erase either. He has to do it completely again. He wants a perfect paper."

"Mostly I'm concerned because I feel we're wasting huge amounts of paper, and also it gets messy after a time. The wastebasket's always overflowing and the floor and the desks are full of it. They ball it up and into the desk it goes. After a while it gets to the point where you can't find the books, in between all the paper."

"It's very hard to get them to understand that they're supposed to conserve paper, that actually we don't have an endless supply. I've given them long lectures on how taxpayers are paying for this. I guess it was just my first reaction, and it wasn't very smart, I admit, so I dropped that. Then I started telling them they couldn't have a second sheet at all; they'd have to make do with their first one. That didn't work, of course, because then, when they messed it up, they had nothing to do and there they were, stuck. Well, then what I did, I used to keep the paper on the counter and all of a sudden, with their wastefulness, the supplies became very short, and I impressed this on the children."

I think this a fair sample of how the teacher's morality (based on the reality principle) requires an economical use of resources but clashes head on with the children's morality (based on the pleasure principle) to the point where no learning takes place. What the teachers failed to realize is that these children, by wasting supplies and asking for more all the time, were trying to find out if the supplies were adequate, if there would be more, even if they didn't grab them now—not to speak of how exciting it was to have one's fill, even if only of clean paper.

Yet it is only on the basis of such pleasurable satiety, with many, many repetitions, and later reflection, that we can afford to postpone, only the teacher wants them to live by this principle before they have learned it. She is critical of their wastefulness, which only reinforces their conviction that "there isn't enough, and we'd better grab it now." So while the children in my example want to learn whether the reality principle is really valid, the teacher prevents their learning it because she wants the learning to have taken place already.

The children's closeness to the pleasure principle reveals itself not only in how they waste paper (which is easily recognized) but also in their need for perfection, in the disbelief that they can correct or erase, because to be able to correct implies the belief that things can be better in the future. It is the very belief that could enable them to move from the pleasure to the reality principle.

I need not tell this readership that the fear they voice when they say "what I don't grab now, I'll never get" has its source in the earliest experiences, particularly those centered around feeding, whether of nutriment or love. I think it of

crucial importance in our efforts to instill the morality
needed for learning that we provide for these children, in
school, those basic experiences on which rests all later
adherence to the reality principle. By this I mean an
abundance of the most basic supplies: food and rest, plus an
emotional supply of acceptance and respect. I think these
children must be taught it is safe to waste—not just paper,
but also food—and that, contrary to past experience in the
home, these will always be in ample supply. It may take a
long time, but eventually all children stop getting bellyaches
from overeating once they feel certain there will be always
enough food to pleasantly fill their stomachs.

I have said that the reality principle, and with it most
learning, has a great deal to do with ego functions and that
the ego must here be supported by moral conscience, since
it cannot rely for this purpose on emotions. But in applying
this realization to education, we again seem stuck with a
conception of the conscience that derives from the
well-integrated middle-class family for whom it works,
though no longer as well as it used to.

Piaget, who studied children at the ages when morality, or
the superego, is developing, concluded that there seem to be
two moralities in childhood, or at least so within the culture
his subjects were drawn from. Developmentally, the earlier
one is a morality of constraint. It is formed in the context of
the one-way relations between the child as the subordinate
and the adult as the dominant person. Its result is a highly
personalized superego, based on having internalized the voice
of very particular persons, chiefly the parents. (Later, if
learning is to proceed smoothly, the teacher will have to be
accepted as a suitable stand-in.) But for that, the parents
had to be very important, very impressive, very dominant, and
—most relevant if we want to understand the predicament
of the underprivileged child—excellent providers.

Soon, however, the child develops further. He becomes

more than just a member of his family; he becomes a member of his society too. Then the morality of constraint is partially replaced by a morality of cooperation, and this is tempered and refined by the spontaneous give and take of peer interaction. At least this is how Piaget describes the development of a conscience in Geneva, Switzerland, a rather conservative and very middle-class city where the heritage of Calvinism is still very strong.

Now in Western society, and particularly in America, relations between child and adult are not so unilateral as they were in Freud's Vienna or Piaget's Geneva. The parent becomes less and less domineering in the child's life, the relations between parent and child less unilateral, and the peer group more important and important much sooner in life—witness the earlier entrance into nursery schools, etc. If this trend continues, then the superego, even for middle-class children, may come to be based essentially on a morality of cooperation with the peer group. Or to use Piaget's central concept, it will be based on having learned to obey the rules of the game.

Now in a consensus society, a conscience based on "obeying the rules of the game," on a "peer group morality," is remarkably unconflicted. Such a conscience is highly concordant with what, in psychoanalysis, are described as two separate, often conflicting, sets of mental functions: those of the ego and the superego—so much so, that where social consensus is high, the two are in many ways identical rather than in conflict. In Geneva, for example, both the peer group morality and that derived from the parents match the morality of society. Ego and superego are then in harmony, and the ego (the soft voice of reason) is not only powerfully supported by the superego but is further strengthened by its success in society. The result is a strong ego. One is well able to live by the reality principle, ready to learn to gain rewards from a society one is very much a part of, ready to follow what the teacher requires, since she almost echoes what one's own superego demands.

This is quite different from a situation in which obeying superego demands that derive from the morality of a particular peer group only puts one at odds with the surrounding community. The values of the teacher are then not recognized as the embodiment of one's own superego, but as an enemy. Clearly they threaten the peer group morality, though that is one's only guide to action, if not to survival itself. In such a case the ego is split apart by trying to satisfy the opposite demands of the peer-group-based superego and those very different ones of the environment.

In our society, even middle-class children are often projected into conflicts like this, and their personality structure is weakened thereby. For example, the sex morality—the rules of the sex game—of a middle-class child as derived from the peer group is much more accepting of instinctual pleasure than is the morality of constraint he derives from his parents. Hence in regard to sex morality the child's superego is often more stringent than a good portion of reality (and hence the ego by itself) would require.

In short, where consensus is low, the more a child has developed his personality on the basis of peer group morality, the less will the teacher succeed with her superego appeals. Then the child's ability to learn will hinge on whether, and how much, his particular peer group supports the demands of education.

From this analysis it becomes clear why our educational system fails the culturally deprived child. He is the child who is deprived of our middle-class culture with its roots in the nuclear family. In his family there is little that supports the reality principle: Opportunities for gratifications not enjoyed at the moment may never recur. No dominant, or at least reliably providing, father figure, fit to be internalized as a superego, is readily available. Thus neither a strong reality principle nor a strong superego is ready to support education. In their stead is a morality that depends almost entirely on the peer group, but a peer group often deeply at odds with the surrounding adult world if not entirely at odds with education as represented by teacher and school.

I could go on, but I think my point has been made. In considering the task of the schools—to instill the morality which is needed for education to reach its goals—we must start out by realizing that the personality of the culturally deprived child is *not* identical with that of the middle-class child. What it contains, in lieu of a personalized morality, is a morality based on his particular subculture and its norms, which as often as not are those of the slums. If we want to activate his interest in education we must appeal to him on the basis of the demands of his own group morality, not ours.

If, therefore, we can offer tangible advantages here and now, both for him and his group and within their particular society, we may be able to reach him. Slowly he may then want to modify his ego ideal, if not also his superego, by moving toward our standards, if only in part.

If it seems that I have not said anything but the well-known "We must start where the child is, and try to guide him to where he should be," that is absolutely right. I have indeed said nothing else.

The catch is that it takes a lot of doing. And if we think that teaching the three R's comes before the morality needed for education, we shall not succeed. Nor will we succeed unless we have first begun with ourselves, where *we* are. The real trick is to rid ourselves of the prejudice of our particular marketplace, because unless we begin there we shall never help the child to give up, however slowly, the prejudice of his own marketplace.

Some time ago, as a matter of fact, I tried my hand at just such a venture when I met with a self-selected group of grade-school teachers who taught mainly lower-class Negro children. At one meeting there had been a heated discussion in which we realized that we must encourage these children not to be quiet in class but to speak up loudly, even in disorderly fashion, because learning to speak up in class about anything they like is a key step toward learning to speak up in class about things the teacher wants them to speak up about. And speaking up on what the teacher wants discussed, even in disorderly ways, is a first step toward heeding her in other ways, such as talking in more orderly fashion. We talked, too, of how the peer group morality (to defy the adult middle-class world) supports their shouting all at once, and of how we, step by step, have to win over that peer group support to where it is more in accord with our morality of doing things in orderly fashion.

As always in life, the situation that soon afterward confronted the teacher was not exactly the one described above. By that time, however, she had learned to apply a principle even where the situation was not at all the same. She told of how all year long she could not get the children to line up quietly when they went out for recess. "Everyday I begged and preached to the children to be quiet and it never worked. But after our last meeting I decided to ignore the bell and pretended to be busy with something at my desk. At first they were as unruly as ever. But after a short time they began to hush each other. 'Shh! Shh!' they said, 'We want to go out.' And I've done that every day since then, all week long, and it's worked like a charm. Once in a while they don't get quiet and I tell them, 'All right. I guess you need a little more time to be noisy.' And pretty soon they get each other quiet."

When I asked this teacher what she thought had happened, she said, "It takes the pressure off me when they put it on each other." And the children can indeed conform when the pressure is from their own peers. This they have learned to respect; it is the pressure from adults they feel they must fight.

Once the teacher begins to think of the pressures the children are under and what she can do about them, instead of worrying about the pressure she herself feels, she will find ways, all on her own, to relieve the children's pressures on her, and everyone is better off. To understand and act on that requires no unusually inspired teachers but only ordinary ones who have been helped to understand what is good for them. And this we can do, when we are no longer bound to our own morality about what is the teacher's role and what is the child's, when we can consider instead what human beings are like, and why they act as they do. Then at least we are free to realize that a lot of satiation has to precede any learning of how to live by the demands of reality, theirs and our own. But by that time their reality and ours are no longer so different.

YOUTH AND VIOLENCE: THE CONTEXTS

OF MORAL CRISIS / *Kenneth Keniston*

If we gather to discuss moral education, it is surely because we sense around us and within us a moral crisis. This crisis is felt at many levels: at the level of international policy, in a world imperiled by weapons that could end all life on this planet; at a national level, in a nation divided over both its priorities and the methods of attaining them; at a political level, in the debate over whether the traditional avenues for the reform of wrong still remain adequate; and at the level of the individual, where more and more men and women feel compelled to decide between the dictates of their own conscience and the laws of their nation.

In any discussion of moral education, then, we should of course consider the general stages in the development of moral reasoning, its alleged familial preconditions, and the logic and technique of moral education. But, in addition, we need to examine the particular moral problems that today concern us and the context in which today's moral dilemmas arise, for morality is not only a matter of how children are brought up, are educated, and learn to reason but—in the crunch—a matter of *what* they believe, *what* they are willing to act on, and *how* they define the world in which they live. Professor Kohlberg's work suggests that many of those who today experience the greatest sense of personal moral crisis are those whose moral reasoning is "postconventional." This level of moral reasoning places them in obvious conflict with the majority of Americans who think in more conventional ways and inevitably confuse post- with preconventional moral thinking.

However illuminating such analyses are, they still do not speak specifically to the urgent sense of moral crisis of our own time. They do not tell us why, in this particular epoch in American (and world) history, the sense of moral crisis should be so intense, nor do they speak to those more specific moral questions, values, and orientations which today seem challenged or which today are used to challenge existing institutions and values. Finally, they do not explain why today the most intense moral challenges to the existing order come from the young.

My comments here are addressed to these more specific questions. They draw upon, but go beyond, observations made upon a small group of young men and women who, in the summer of 1967, led an antiwar organization called Vietnam Summer.[1] My chief concern in that research was to understand the psychological process whereby these young men and women had come to think of themselves as radicals. As the study progressed, two issues became clear. First, for these young radicals, moral issues were at the heart of their concern, and their fundamental criticism of American policies, institutions, and values was a moral one. Second, their lives could only be understood in the context of the history of the postwar world, which had created new opportunities and new dilemmas for all of the members of their generation. The effort to understand this historical context and to formulate the major values and antivalues upon which these young radicals stood led to the speculations which follow.

THE PSYCHOHISTORICAL IMPACT OF THE POSTWAR ERA

Perhaps the main characteristic of the postwar era has been the *breakneck pace of change* in virtually every area of life, thought, and social organization. The last two decades have been a time of "radical" and "revolutionary" world upheaval, and although the changes in American society have been less dramatic and violent, they have been equally thoroughgoing. The mere fact of social change, of the continual alteration of the physical, human, and intellectual environment, is itself a major determinant of the lives of this postwar generation. For now, consider some of the specific changes which have occurred.

Hanging over the lives of all men and women during the past decade have been the Bomb and the terrifying possibilities of *technological death* it summarizes and symbolizes. These include not only holocaustal destruction by thermonuclear blast and radiation but the possibility of slower forms of technological death from deliberately destructive biochemical interventions in the human ecology. To be sure, the possibility of premature and unannounced death has always been a fearful constant in human life. What is new about technological death is not only that it is quantitatively more violent and destructive than any previously imagined human invention but that it is mechanical, impersonal, automatic, and absurd. One well-intentioned man (who means no harm and is only following orders) can press a button and set in motion a chain of events which could mean the burning, maiming, and gruesome death of most of those now alive. This possibility has been a constant backdrop to the development of a whole generation, incorporated into their lives not only in childhood terrors of the Bomb but in the routine experience of air raid drills in school, in constant exposure to discussion of fallout shelters, ballistic missiles and antimissile defenses, and sometimes in a compulsive fascination with and terror of the technology of destruction. There are relatively few young Americans who, upon hearing a distant explosion, seeing a bright flash, or hearing a far away sound of jets overhead at night, have not wondered for a brief instant whether this might not be "It."

A second crucial change in the past two decades is the still incomplete process of decolonization, the *revolutionary liberation of the oppressed,* exploited, and largely nonwhite majority of the world. As seen through the early recollections of young white Americans, this issue involves Negro Americans. For most young Americans, involvement in the American version of the worldwide liberation of the oppressed begins in childhood or adolescence, when they "naturally"

identified with the efforts of young Negro students to demand
dignity and respect, whether it was witnessing the early sit-ins
and freedom rides on television, participating vicariously in
the Little Rock demonstrations, or rejoicing in the Supreme
Court decision of 1954. Many young Americans have become
directly or vicariously involved with the civil rights
movement. And when recently they were called upon to fight
against the movement of national liberation in Southeast
Asia, the reaction of at least some was to identify American
intervention with the spirit of southern sheriffs and prejudiced
northerners, siding with the anticolonial nationalistic
nonwhite forces of revolution in Vietnam, caring little
whether these forces were communists.

Still another development in advanced societies is what
might be termed the *technologization of life*. Terms like
automation, rationalization, and bureaucratization suggest
the sociologist's analysis of these developments; concepts
like objectification, depersonalization, and massification are
the social critic's response to them. But no matter how we
characterize or respond to them, the trends of the last two
decades are clearly apparent: increasing bigness in
government, the military, education, weaponry, automobiles,
and cities; increasingly complex and differentiated organization in all areas in American life; a steady growth in the
automation and computerization of many activities and
decisions once reserved, for better or worse, for human
beings.

Such trends have their personal effects. Some young
radicals witnessed directly their parents' effort to prosper or
even to survive in a society increasingly complex, increasingly
organized, increasingly demanding of highly developed
technical skills. Many felt concretely in their secondary
schools and colleges what largeness and bureaucratization
can mean; almost without exception, they had struggled to
avoid being a "number" and insisted upon being treated as
individuals. Furthermore, they are members of a generation

raised on the corrosive skepticism of *Mad Magazine*, taught paradoxically by television to be skeptical of commercial claims, reared during their preadolescent and adolescent years in the era of Togetherness, which denied but did not conceal the rifts in American life. Thoughtful, articulate, and principled young men and women, taught from an early age by most of their families that there was more to life than "success" and remuneration, and surrounded by a technology in which they saw frightening possibilities of impersonality, they began in late adolescence to challenge the impersonality, dehumanization, overorganization, and commercialization of American life.

Finally, these young men and women grew up in an era of uninterrupted and *automatic affluence*. For most young men and women of middle-class backgrounds, the fact of affluence has been simply taken for granted. Although one or two of those interviewed came from lower middle-class homes and considered themselves "poor" during their childhoods, none ever had to worry about food, clothing, or adequate education, nor even about a television set, a family car, and a vacation every year. When the time came for them to consider adult commitments, the question of income, social status, upward mobility, or finding a job had virtually no relevance. And when they realized at some point in their youth that the affluence they took for granted had not been extended to all Americans, much less to the impoverished two-thirds of the world, they reacted with outrage and dismay. In an affluent era, radicals (who almost always come from the middle class) show less guilt and more outrage at poverty: they do not feel ashamed of their own prosperity but angry at the system that still excludes others from a share in it.

In all these areas, the distant historical backdrop of individual life was also the ground on which it occurred. Breakneck social change, technological destructiveness, the revolution of the oppressed, new techniques of communication, the technologization of life, and the fact of automatic affluence were not merely the distant scenery of this generation's development but its stuff and substance. For these young radicals, unusually identified with historical events, the terms "radical" and "revolutionary" are descriptive not only of themselves but of the world in which they have always lived, and while the radical changes and revolutions I have discussed often seem impersonally caused, it is not surprising that these young men and women might determine personally to effect changes no less radical or revolutionary.

In the modern world, there are of course vast and important cultural and national differences. Yet in other respects, the experience of youth in all nations is becoming increasingly similar: the same historical events affect and shape all, and similar youth phenomena are apparent in a variety of nations, advanced and developing. Sometimes to greater and sometimes to lesser degree, the revolutions that have affected American youth have affected their contemporaries elsewhere. We are moving toward a world in which there is only one history—world history.

THE POSTMODERN STYLE

The great majority of young Americans in their early twenties are not radicals, nor dissenters, protesters, or activists, nor alienated hippies, bohemians, or beatniks. So it is only as a speculation that we can generalize from radical and dissenting youth to other youth, and then always with the proviso that we are speaking of a morally conscious minority, which, although it helps set the tone and style of its generation, constitutes but a small part of that age group.

In emphasizing "style" rather than ideology, identity, traits, objectives, or characteristics, I mean to suggest that the communalities in postmodern youth are to be found in the *way* in which they approach the world rather than in their actual behavior, ideologies, or goals. Indeed, the focus upon "process" rather than program is perhaps the prime characteristic of the postmodern style, reflecting a world in which process and change are more obvious than purpose and goal. For, as I will suggest, postmodern youth, at least in America, are themselves very much in process, unfinished in their development, deliberately open to a historically unpredictable future. In such a world, where ideologies come and go, and where revolutionary change is the rule, a "style," a *way* of doing things, is more possible to maintain than any more fixed goals or constancies of behavior.

In contemporary American society, the style of postmodern youth is best illustrated in the New Left and the hippies, informal youth groups which in their combined active membership constitute but a small percentage of their generation, although they are already giving a distinctive imprint to their contemporaries. There are many important psychological, social, political, and ideological differences between the hippie and the more activist radical. But, beyond these important differences, hippies and radicals have in common visible discomfort with existing American society and an often agonized search for ways to change or escape this society. Moreover, both hippies and young radicals tend to be drawn from similar backgrounds: upper middle-class, politically liberal secular families, excellent educations, and attendance at prestigious colleges.

Fluidity of Identity. Postmodern youth display a special personal and psychological openness, flexibility, and incompleteness. Even the term "identity" suggests a greater fixity, stability, and "closure" than most young radicals in fact possess. Indeed, it seems possible that the traditional description of identity development may need to be changed to allow for the impact of social change upon elite youth. No longer is it possible to speak of the normal "resolution" of identity issues, and our earlier fear of the ominous implications of "prolonged adolescence" must now be qualified by an awareness that in postmodern youth many "adolescent" issues and qualities persist long past the time when in earlier eras they "should" have ended. Increasingly, the identity development of postmodern youth is tied to social and historical changes which have not occurred and which may never occur. Thus, psychological "closure," shutting doors and burning bridges, becomes impossible. The concept of the personal future and the "life work" are ever more hazily defined; the effort to change oneself, redefine oneself, or reform oneself does not cease with the arrival of biological adulthood.

This fluidity and openness extends through all areas of life. Both hippie and New Left movements are nondogmatic, nonideological, and to a large extent hostile to doctrine and formula. In the New Left, the focus is on "tactics," amongst hippies, on simple direct acts of love and communication. In neither group does one find clear-cut, long-range social and political plans or life patterns laid out in advance. The vision of the personal and collective future is blurred and vague: later adulthood is left deliberately open. In neither group is psychological development considered complete; in both groups, identity, like history, is fluid and indeterminate. In one sense, of course, identity development takes place; but in another sense, identity is never finally achieved but is always undergoing transformations that parallel the transformations of the historical world.

Generational Identification. Postmodern youth view themselves primarily as a part of a generation rather than as an organization; they identify with their contemporaries as a group, rather than with elders; and they do not have clearly defined leaders and heroes. Their deepest collective identification is to their own group or "Movement"—a term that in its ambiguous meanings points not only to the fluidity and openness of postmodern youth but to their physical mobility and the absence of traditional patterns of leadership and emulation.

And although postmodern youth are often widely read in the "literature" of the New Left or consciousness-expansion, no one person or set of people is central to their intellectual beliefs. Although they live together in groups, these groups are without clear leaders. Generations today are separated by a very brief span, and the individual's own phase of youthful usefulness, for example as hippie or as organizer, is limited to a relatively few years. Generations come and go quickly; whatever is to be accomplished must therefore be done soon.

Generational consciousness also entails a feeling of psychological disconnection from previous generations, their life situations, and their ideologies. Among young radicals, there is a strong feeling that the older ideologies are exhausted or irrelevant, expressed in detached amusement at the doctrinaire disputes of the "old Left" and impatience with "old liberals." Among hippies, the irrelevance of the parental past is even greater; if there is any source of insight, it is the timeless tradition of the East, not the values of the previous generation in American society. But in both groups, the central values are those created in the present by the "Movement" itself.

Personalism. Both groups are highly personalistic in their styles of relationship. Among hippies, personalism usually entails privatism, a withdrawal from efforts to be involved in or to change the wider social world; among young radicals, personalism is joined with efforts to change the world. But despite this difference, both groups care most deeply about the creation of intimate, loving, open, and trusting relationships between small groups of people. The ultimate judge of man's life is the quality of his personal relationship; the greatest sin, what sends people into psychotherapy, is to be unable to relate to others in a direct, face-to-face, one-to-one relationship.

The obverse of personalism is the discomfort created by any nonpersonal, "objectified," professionalized, and above all exploitative relationship. Manipulation, power relationships, superordination, control, and domination are at violent odds with the I-thou mystique. Failure to treat others as fully human, inability to enter into personal relationships with them, is viewed with dismay in others and with guilt in oneself. Even with opponents the goal is to establish confrontations in which the issues can be discussed openly.

Nonasceticism. Postmodern youth are nonascetic, expressive, and sexually free. The sexual openness of the hippie world has been much discussed and criticized in the mass media. One finds a similar sexual and expressive freedom among many young radicals, although it is less provocatively demonstrative. In the era of the Pill, responsible sexual expression becomes increasingly possible outside of marriage, at the same time that sexuality becomes less laden with guilt, fear, and prohibition. As asceticism disappears, so does promiscuity: the personalism of postmodern youth requires that sexual expression must occur in the context of "meaningful" human relationships, of intimacy and mutuality. Marriage is increasingly seen as an institution for having children, but sexual relationships are viewed as the natural concomitant of close relationships between the sexes. What is important is not sexual activity itself but the context in which it occurs. Sex is right and natural between people who are "good to each other," but sexual exploitation —failure to treat one's partner as a person—is strongly disapproved.

Antitechnologism. Postmodern youth have grave reservations about many of the technological aspects of the contemporary world. The depersonalization of life, commercialism, careerism, and familialism, the bureaucratization and complex organization of advanced nations—all seem intolerable to these young men and women, who seek to create new forms of association and action to oppose the technologism of our day. Bigness, impersonality, stratification, and hierarchy are rejected, as is any involvement with the furtherance of technological values. In reaction to these values, postmodern youth seek simplicity, naturalness, personhood, and even voluntary poverty.

But a revolt against technologism is, of course, only possible in a technological society, and to be effective, it must inevitably exploit technology to overcome technologism. Thus in postmodern youth, the fruits of technology— synthetic hallucinogens in the hippie subculture, modern technology of communication among young radicals—and the affluence made possible by technological society are a precondition for a postmodern style. The demonstrative poverty of the hippie would be meaningless in a society where poverty is routine; for the radical to work for subsistence wages as a matter of choice is to *have* a choice not available in most parts of the world. Furthermore, to "organize" against the pernicious aspects of the technological era requires high skill in the use of modern technologies of organization: the long distance telephone, the mass media, high speed travel, and so on. In the end, then, it is not the material but the spiritual consequences of technology that postmodern youth oppose. What *is* adamantly rejected is the contamination of life with the values of technological organization and production. A comparable rejection of the psychological consequences of current technology, coupled with the simultaneous ability to to exploit that technology, probably characterizes all dissenting groups in all epochs.

Participation. Postmodern youth are committed to a search for new forms of groups, of organizations, and of action where decision-making is collective, arguments are resolved by "talking them out," and where self-examination, interpersonal criticism, and group decision-making are fused. The objective is to create new styles of life and new types of organization that humanize rather than dehumanize, that activate and strengthen the participants rather than undermining or weakening them. And the primary vehicle for such participation is the small, face-to-face primary group of peers.

The search for new participatory forms of organization and action can hardly be deemed successful as yet, especially in the New Left, where effectiveness in the wider social and political scene remains to be demonstrated. But there may yet evolve from the hippie "tribes" small Digger communities, and from primary groups of the New Left new forms of association in which self-criticism, awareness of group interaction, and the accomplishment of social and political goals go hand in hand. The effort to create groups in which individuals grow from their participation in the group extends far beyond the New Left and the hippie world; the same search is seen in the widespread enthusiasm for "sensitivity training" groups and even in the increasing use of groups as a therapeutic instrument. Nor is this solely an American search: one sees a similar focus, for example, in the communist nations, with their emphasis on small groups which engage in the "struggle" of mutual criticism and self-criticism.

The search for effectiveness combined with participation has also led to the evolution of "new" forms of social and political action. The newness of such forms of political action as parades and demonstrations is open to some question; perhaps what is most new is the *style* in which old forms of social action are carried out. The most consistent effort is to force one's opponent into a personal confrontation with one's own point of view. Sit-ins, freedom rides, insistence upon discussions, silent and nonviolent demonstrations and confrontations—all have a prime objective to "get through to" the other side, to force reflection, to bear witness as an existential act, and to impress upon others the sincerity and validity of one's own principles. There is much that is old and familiar about this. Yet the underlying purpose of many of the emerging forms of social and political action, whether they are "human be-ins," "love-ins," peace marches, confrontations, resistance, or "teach-ins," has a new flavor —hope that by expressing one's own principles, by "demonstrating" one's convictions, one can lure one's opponents into participating with one's own values.

Anti-Academicism. Among postmodern youth, one finds a virtually unanimous rejection of the "merely academic." This rejection is one manifestation of a wider insistence on the relevance, applicability, and personal meaningfulness of knowledge. It would be wrong simply to label this trend "anti-intellectual," for most new radicals and some hippies are themselves highly intellectual people. What *is* demanded is that intelligence be engaged with the world, just as action should be informed by knowledge.

To postmodern youth, much of what is taught in schools, colleges, and universities is largely irrelevant to living life in the last third of the twentieth century. Some academics are seen as indirect apologists for the Organized System in the United States. Much of what they teach is considered simply unconnected to the experience of postmodern youth. New ways of learning are sought, ways that combine action with reflection, ways that fuse engagement in the world with understanding of it. In an era of rapid change, the accrued wisdom of the past is cast into question, and youth seeks not only new knowledge but new ways of arriving at knowledge.

Nonviolence. Finally, postmodern youth of all persuasions meet on the ground of nonviolence. For hippies, the avoidance of and calming of violence is a central objective, symbolized by gifts of flowers to policemen and the slogan "Make love, not war." And although nonviolence as a philosophical principle has lost most of its power in the New Left, nonviolence as a psychological orientation remains a crucial —perhaps *the* crucial—issue for most. The nonviolence of postmodern youth should not be confused with pacifism: these are not necessarily young men and women who believe in turning the other cheek or who are systematically opposed to fighting for what they believe in. But the basic style of both radicals and hippies is profoundly opposed to warfare, destruction, and exploitation of man by man and to violence whether on an interpersonal or an international scale.

THE CREDIBILITY GAP: PRINCIPLE AND PRACTICE

In considering the historical context for the development of postmodern youth, I have emphasized the massive and violent social changes of the past two decades. The social changes of the past generation affect the young in a variety of ways: in particular, they contribute to a special sensitivity to the discrepancy between principle and practice. For during this era of rapid social change, the values most deeply internalized in the parental generation and expressed in their behavior in time of crisis are frequently very different from the more "modern" principles, ideals, and values which this generation has professed and attempted to practice in bringing up its children. Filial perception of the discrepancy between practice and principle may help explain the special sensitivity amongst postmodern youth to the "hypocrisy" of the previous generation.

The grandparents of today's twenty-year-olds were generally born at the end of the nineteenth century and were brought up during the pre-World War I years. Heirs of a Victorian tradition as yet unaffected by the value revolutions of the twentieth century, they reared their own children, the parents of today's youth, in families that emphasized respect, the control of impulse, obedience to authority, and the traditional "inner-directed" values of hard work, deferred gratification, and self-restraint. Their children, born around the time of the first World War, were thus socialized in families that remained largely Victorian in outlook.

During their lifetime, however, these parents (and in particular the most intelligent and advantaged among them) were exposed to a great variety of new values which often changed their nominal faiths. During their youth in the 1920's and 1930's, major changes in American behavior and American values took place. The 1920's and the 1930's were an era when older Victorian values were challenged, attacked, and all but discredited, especially in educated middle-class families. Young men and women who went to college during this period (as did most of the parents of those who can be termed postmodern today) were influenced outside their families by a variety of "progressive," "liberal," and even psychoanalytic ideas that contrasted sharply with the values of their childhood families. Moreover, during the 1930's, many of the parents of today's upper middle-class youth were exposed to or involved with the ideals of the New Deal and sometimes to more radical interpretations of man, society, and history. Finally, in the 1940's and 1950's, when it came time to rear their own children, the parents of today's elite youth were strongly influenced by "permissive" views of child-rearing that again contrasted sharply with the techniques by which they themselves had been raised. Thus, many middle-class parents moved during their lifetime from the Victorian ethos in which they had been socialized to the less moralistic, more humanitarian, and more "expressive" values of their own adulthoods.

But major changes in values, when they occur in adult life, are likely to be far from complete. To have grown up in a family where unquestioning obedience to parents was expected, but to rear one's own children in an atmosphere of "democratic" permissiveness and self-determination—and never to revert to the practices of one's own childhood—

requires a change of values more total and comprehensive than most adults can achieve. Furthermore, behavior which springs from values acquired in adulthood often appears somewhat forced, artificial, or insincere to the sensitive observer. Children, clearly the most sensitive observers of their own parents, are likely to sense a discrepancy between their parents' avowed and consciously held values and their "basic instincts" with regard to child-rearing. Furthermore, the parental tendency to "revert to form" is greatest in times of family crisis, which are of course the times that have the weightiest effect upon children.

In a time of rapid social change, then, a special "credibility gap" is likely to open between the generations. Children are likely to perceive a considerable discrepancy between what the parents avow as their values and the actual assumptions from which parental behavior springs. In the young radicals interviewed, for example, the focal issue of adolescent rebellion against parents seem to have been just this discrepancy, the children arguing that their parents' endorsement of independence and self-determination for their children was "hypocritical" in that it did not correspond with the real behavior of the parents when their children actually sought independence. Similar perceptions of "hypocrisy" occurred for others around racial matters; for example, there were a few parents who in principle supported racial and religious equality but who became violently upset when their children dated someone from another race or religion.

Of course, no society ever fully lives up to its own professed ideals. In every society, there is a gap between credal values and actual practices, and in every society the recognition of this gap constitutes a powerful motor for social change. But in most societies, especially when social change is slow and institutions are powerful and unchanging, there occurs what we might term the "institutionalization of hypocrisy." Children and adolescents routinely learn when it is "reasonable" to expect that the values people profess will be implemented in their behavior and when it is not reasonable. There develops an elaborate system of commentary upon the society's credal values, excluding certain people or situations from the full weight of these values or "demonstrating" that apparent inconsistencies are not really inconsistencies at all. Thus, in almost all societies, a "sincere" man who "honestly" believes one set of values is frequently allowed to ignore them completely, for example, in the practice of his business, in many interpersonal relationships, in dealings with foreigners, in relationships to his children, and so on—all because these areas have been officially defined as exempt from the application of his credal values.

In a time of rapid social change and value change, however, the institutionalization of hypocrisy seems to break down. "New" values have been in existence for so brief a period that the exemptions to them have not yet been defined, the situations to be excluded have not yet been determined, and the universal gap between principle and practice appears in all of its nakedness. The mere fact of a discrepancy between social values and social practice is not at all unusual. But what is special about the present situation of rapid value change is, first, that parents themselves tend to have two conflicting sets of values—one related to the experience of their early childhood, the other to the ideologies and principles acquired in adulthood—and, second, that no stable institutions or rules for defining hypocrisy out of existence have yet been fully evolved. In such a situation, children see the emperor's nakedness with unusual clarity, recognizing the value conflict within their parents and perceiving clearly the hypocritical gap between creed and behavior.

This points to one of the central characteristics of postmodern youth: they insist on taking seriously a great variety of political, personal, and social principles which "no one in his right mind" ever before thought of attempting to extend to dealings with strangers, relations between the races, or international politics. For example, peaceable openness has long been a credal virtue in our society, but it has never been extended to foreigners, particularly those with dark skins. Similarly, equality has long been preached, but the "American dilemma" has been resolved by a series of institutionalized hypocrisies which exempted Negroes from the application of this principle. Love has always been a central value in Christian society, but really to love one's enemies—to be generous to policemen, customers, criminals, servants, or foreigners—has been considered folly.

These speculations on the credibility gap between the generations in a time of rapid change may help explain two crucial facts about postmodern youth: first, they frequently come from highly principled families with whose principles they continue to agree; second, that they have the outrageous temerity to insist that individuals and societies live by the values they preach.

VIOLENCE: SADISM AND CATACLYSM

The issue of violence is central not only for young radicals but for postmodern youth the world over. Recall, once again, some of the early memories of the young radicals interviewed: the destructiveness of the atomic bomb, a menacing tank grinding over the rubble of war, a man escaping from a threatening mob, a man being struck in the face, the exploitation of the darker-skinned by the white. In all of these memories, issues of violence are central; in each of them, violence without finds echo and counterpart in the violence of inner feelings. The term "violence" suggests both of these possibilities: the *psychological* violence of sadism, exploitation, and aggression and the *historical* violence of war, cataclysm, and holocaust. In the lives of young radicals, as of most of their generation, the threats of inner and outer violence are fused, each activating, exciting, and potentiating the other. To summarize a complex thesis into a few words: *the issue of violence is to this generation what the issue of sex was to the Victorian world.*

Stated differently, what is most deeply repressed, rejected, feared, controlled, and projected onto others by the postmodern generation is no longer their own sexuality. Sex, for most of this generation, is much freer, more open, and less guilt- and anxiety-ridden than it was for previous generations. But violence, whether in one's self or in others, has assumed new prominence as the prime source of inner and outer terror. That this should be so in the modern world is readily understandable. Over all of us hangs the continual threat of a technological violence more meaningless, absurd, premature, total, and unpremeditated than any ever imagined before. I have stressed the resonance of individual life with historical change, emphasizing that history is not merely the backdrop for human development but its ground. To be grounded in the history of the past two decades is to have stood upon, to have lived amidst, to have experienced, both directly and vicariously, violent upheaval, violent worldwide revolution, and the unrelenting possibility of worldwide destruction. To have been alive and aware in America during the past decade has been to be exposed to the assassination of a president and the televised murder of his alleged murderer, to the well-publicized slaughter of Americans by their mad fellow countrymen, and to the recent violence in our cities. To have been a middle-class child in the past two decades is to have watched daily the violence of television, both as it reports the bloodshed and turmoil of the American and non-American world and as it skillfully elaborates and externalizes in repetitive dramas the potential for violence within each of us.

It therefore requires no assumption of an increase in biological aggressivity to account for the salience of the issue of violence for postmodern youth. The capacity for rage, spite, and aggression is part of our endowment as human beings: it is a constant potential of human nature. But during the past two decades—indeed, starting before World War II—we have both witnessed and imagined violence on a scale more frightening than ever before. Like the angry child who fears that his rage alone will destroy those around him, we have become vastly more sensitive to and fearful of our inner angers, for we live in a world where even the mildest irritation, multiplied a billionfold by modern technology, might destroy all civilization. The fact of violent upheaval and the possibility of cataclysm has been literally brought into our living rooms during the past twenty years: it has been interwoven with the development of a whole generation.

In studying young antiwar radicals, I was impressed by the many themes and tensions, psychological, interpersonal, and organizational, that were related to the issue of violence. The avoidance, elimination, and control of violence, whether in the form of warfare, naked aggression, or exploitation of others, is a central goal and psychological orientation in the New Left. Some of the special dilemmas of the New Left seem related to the zealous and systematic effort to avoid any action or relationship in which inner or outer violence may be evoked. The consistent efforts made to avoid domination within the Movement and to eliminate all manipulation in the world at large, like the distrust of authority, the avoidance of leadership lest it lead to domination, the hostility to "flashiness" in political activities lest it lead to exploitation—all seem related to the avoidance of violence. So do the deliberate efforts of many young radicals to overcome their own angers and aggressions, their remarkable ability to retain control when provoked, their basic preference for "nonviolent" forms of protest and action, and their largely successful struggle to overcome in themselves any conscious vestige of exploitiveness, aggression, or manipulation in human relations.

I do not mean to suggest that student radicals in particular or postmodern youth in general are tight-lipped pacifists, rage-filled deniers of their own inner angers. On the contrary, exuberance, passionateness, and zest are the rule rather than the exception, and young radicals are not incapable of anger, rage, and resentment, especially when their principles are violated. But perhaps more than most, they learned early in their lives the fruitlessness of conflict; and this lesson, in later years, was among the many intertwined forces that went into their decisions to work for Vietnam Summer.

To many young people of this generation, the avoidance of violence is central. In the goals within the New Left, the end of warfare, exploitation, and domination is central; within the Movement itself, the search for new forms of social organization and political action that avoid manipulation, oppression, and control is crucial; and within young radicals themselves, the struggle to overcome, sublimate, or rechannel their tendencies to anger, rage, and destructiveness constitutes a unifying theme. In this last endeavor, the young men and women I interviewed had been largely successful, probably because whatever inner disposition to violence they possessed has been channeled into "aggressive" efforts to create outlooks and institutions that would bring an end to personal, social, and political violence.

In pointing to the psychological dimension of the issue of violence, I do not mean to attribute causal primacy to either the experiences of early life or their residues in adulthood. My thesis is rather that for those of this generation who possess the greatest historical awareness, the psychological and historical possibilities of violence have come to potentiate each other. To repeat: witnessing the acting out of violence on a scale more gigantic than ever before, or imaginatively participating in the possibility of worldwide holocaust, activates the fear of one's own violence; heightened awareness of one's inner potential for rage, anger, or destructiveness increases one's sensitivity to the possibility of violence in the world.

This same process of historical activation of inner violence has occurred, I believe, throughout the modern world and brings with it not only the intensified efforts to curb violence we see in this small segment of postmodern youth but other more frightening possibilities. These young radicals, to an unusual degree, remained open to and aware of their own angers and aggressions, and this awareness created in them a sufficient understanding of inner violence to enable them to control it in themselves and oppose it in others. Most men and women, young or old, possess less insight: their inner sadism is projected onto others whom they thereafter loathe or abjectly serve; or, more disastrously, historically heightened inner violence is translated into outer aggression and murderousness, sanctioned by self-righteousness.

In underlining the issue of violence, I am pointing to one of the central dimensions in the sense of moral crisis experienced by modern men and women. The brief years that have ensued since the antiwar organizing efforts of Vietnam Summer 1967 have illustrated even more clearly the centrality of this issue, both for those who oppose violence and for those who are themselves violent. Even the opponent of violence constantly risks resorting to violence in order to end violence and thereby creating or exciting more violence than he undoes. Moreover, these few years have underlined even more impressively man's psychological capacity and technological ability violently to destroy his fellow man and the immense problems in knowing how best to oppose and counteract these violent trends.

If there is any conclusion to be drawn from these reflections, it might best be stated as a footnote to Professor Kohlberg's remarks on justice. Perhaps Kohlberg may well be correct in suggesting that all values are united, ultimately, in the concept of justice. Yet insofar as justice can be done, it can only be done in a world in which there is life. It may be, then, that the preservation of life—its furtherance, development, and nurture—is a principle even more fundamental than justice, for without life the issue of justice cannot arise. And it may be that our current sense of moral crisis is animated by our shared (if largely unstated) fear that man has today created the instruments whereby the life of man has been placed in jeopardy. Thus, I would maintain that the question that today underlies our distinct approaches to the question of moral education is the question of how to create new formulations and forms to control man's potential to destroy himself.

NOTES

EDUCATION FOR MORAL RESPONSIBILITY

1. *Meno*, 70A, Jowett translation.

2. F. A. Olafson, *Principles and Persons* (Baltimore, Johns Hopkins Press, 1967), p. xiv.

3. For an earlier development of the general thrust of this paragraph in relation to Christian ethical literature, see my "Context vs. Principles: A Misplaced Debate in Christian Ethics," *Harvard Theological Review*, 58 (1965), 171–202.

4. The literature which informs a more elaborate and precise delineation of a theory of action is vast. A sampling might consist of the following:

Hannah Arendt, *The Human Condition* (Chicago, University of Chicago Press, 1958); John MacMurray, *The Self as Agent* (New York, Harper, 1957); John MacMurray, *Persons in Relations* (New York, Harper, 1961); H. R. Niebuhr, *The Responsible Self* (New York, Harper and Row, 1963); G. E. M. Anscombe, *Intention*, 2nd ed. (Oxford, B. Blackwell, 1963); S. Hampshire, *Thought and Action* (New York, Viking, 1960); E. D'arcy, *Human Acts* (Oxford, the Clarendon Press, 1963); R. Taylor, *Action and Purpose* (Englewood Cliffs, N.J., Prentice-Hall, 1966); R. S. Peters, *The Concept of Motivation* (London, Routledge & Kegan Paul, 1961); A. Kenny, *Action, Emotion and Will* (London, Routledge & Kegan Paul, 1963); P. Ricoeur, *Freedom and Nature: The Voluntary and the Involuntary* (Evanston, Ill., Northwestern University Press, 1966); *Toward a General Theory of Action*, ed. T. Parsons and E. Shils (Cambridge, Mass., Harvard University Press, 1952).

Also there are many articles dealing with the issues, e.g., by H. L. A. Hart, Roderick Chisholm, J. L. Austin, and others.

5. For a study of the claimed significance of religious beliefs about Jesus Christ for moral life, see my *Christ and the*

Moral Life (New York, Harper and Row, 1968). The
last chapter states a constructive position on the issue.

6. N. Hartmann, *Ethics*, vol. II; *Moral Values* (London,
Allen and Unwin, 1932), p. 189.

7. Ibid., p. 226.

8. Luke 10: 25–37. See Sallie McFague TeSelle, *Literature
and the Christian Life* (New Haven, Conn., Yale University
Press, 1967), for a more extensive study of this point.

All Biblical quotations are from the Revised Standard
Version of the Bible.

CONCRETE PRINCIPLES

1. A. MacIntyre, *A Short History of Ethics* (London,
Routledge & Kegan Paul, 1967).

2. See ibid., pp. 95–96.

3. H. L. Hart, *The Concept of Law* (London, Oxford
University Press, 1961), chaps. viii, ix.

4. See M. Oakeshott, "The Tower of Babel," in *Rationalism
in Politics* (London, Methuen, 1962).

5. London, Allen and Unwin, 1966.

6. For fuller treatment of the concept of "character"
see R. S. Peters, "Moral Education and the Psychology of
Character," *Philosophy* (January 1962); reprinted in *Philosophy and Education*, 2nd ed., ed. I. Scheffler (Boston, Allyn
and Bacon, 1966).

7. It might well be asked whether any kind of priority is
to be given to one or other of these distinct elements in
the moral life. Are a man's motives in performing a role
morally more crucial than the efficiency with which he per-
forms it? Are his ideals, deriving from his concept of the
good, more or less important than his adherence to
interpersonal rules? Can "duty" be reconciled with "interest"?
Are higher order traits, such as determination and integrity,
to be admired irrespective of the purposes a man pursues
or the rule he follows? The devil, according to all accounts,
is damnably persistent. Is it possible to discern any
rational unity in a moral life which emphasizes the importance

of man as a person and not just as an occupant of a role?
Or is MacIntyre right in thinking that such a moral life must
necessarily be schizophrenic? These are difficult questions
whose answer can be sought only by going into details
of moral philosophy.

8. For extensive treatment of fundamental principles
see Peters, *Ethics and Education,* chaps. iv, vi, vii, viii.

9. See S. C. Toulmin, *The Place of Reason in Ethics*
(Cambridge, Cambridge University Press, 1950), chap. 11.

10. See Peters, "Education and the Educated Man," in
*Proceedings of the Philosophy of Education Society of Great
Britain,* January 1970.

11. For further treatment of this interpersonal realm
of morality in relation to stages of child development see R. S.
Peters, "Reason and Habit: The Paradox of Moral Education,"
in *Moral Education in a Changing Society,* ed. W. R.
Niblett (London, Faber, 1963); reprinted in *Philosophy and
Education,* 2nd ed., ed. I Scheffler (Boston, Allyn and
Bacon, 1966).

12. Spinoza, *Ethics,* part V., prop. XLII.

EDUCATION FOR JUSTICE

1. Boston, Houghton Mifflin, 1967.

2. W. Ball, "Post-Schemp," in *Religion and Public Education,* ed. T. Sizer (Boston, Houghton Mifflin, 1967).

3. For a recent example of this line of thought, see a piece
by William F. Buckley, Jr., in the *New York Times
Magazine,* November 28, 1967, Symposium on Civil
Disobedience and Vietnam, "For Some Deportment, Deportation." "It ought to be the individual's right to go along with
his community, but the community not the individual should
specify the consequences. For those who ask to retain a
personal veto over every activity of their Government, whether
it is a war in Vietnam or the social or educational policies
of a municipal administration, are asking for the kind of lati-
tude which breaks the bonds of civil society. The consequence
for studied and aggravated civil disobedience seem to me

obvious, deportation. Ideally of course, a citizen whose disagreements with his country are organic should take the initiative and seek out more compatible countries." Other statements by eminent people in this symposium are examples of Stages 4, 5, and 6.

4. S. Milgram, "Behavioral Study of Obedience," *Journal of Abnormal Social Psychology*, 67 (1963), 371–378.

5. N. Haan, M. Smith, and J. Block, "The Moral Reasoning of Young Adults: Political-Social Behavior, Family Background and Personality Correlates," *Journal of Personality and Social Psychology*, 10 (1968), 183–201.

6. M. Blatt and L. Kohlberg, "The Effects of Classroom Discussion on Moral Reasoning," in *Research on Moralization, The Cognitive-Developmental Approach*, ed. Kohlberg and Turiel (New York, Holt, Rinehart & Winston, to be published).

7. The Meeting School in Rindge, New Hampshire.

MORAL EDUCATION

1. D. P. Moynihan, "Education of the Urban Poor," *Harvard Graduate School of Education Association Bulletin*, 12, no. 2 (1967), 6.

2. Herbert R. Kohl, *36 Children* (New York, New American Library), 1967.

3. Sylvia Ashton-Warner, *The Spinster* (London, Secker Warburg), 1958, and *The Teacher* (New York, Simon and Schuster), 1963.

YOUTH AND VIOLENCE

1. See Keniston, *Young Radicals* (New York, Harcourt, Brace and World, 1968).

DATE DUE

DEC 1 6 1971		
MR 26 72		
AP 1 1 73		
AP 2 5 73		
MAY 2 0 1973		
JUL 2 6 1973		
1975		
OC 3 0 '75		
NU 1 3 '75		
MAY 1 0 1978		
MAR 17 1980		
MAY 1 8 1982		
NOV 8 1982		
MAY 1 6		
MAY 2 3 1984		
MAY 1 1985		
DEC 8 97		
GAYLORD		PRINTED IN U.S.A.